CASALS
AND THE ART
OF
INTERPRETATION

DAVID BLUM

With
An Introduction by Paul Tortelier
and
A Foreword by Antony Hopkins

UNIVERSITY OF CALIFORNIA PRESS
BERKELEY AND LOS ANGELES

University of California Press
Berkeley and Los Angeles, California

© David Blum 1977

First California Paperback Edition 1980

Library of Congress Cataloging in Publication Data

Blum, David.
    Casals and the art of interpretation.

    Includes index.
    1. Casals, Pablo, 1876–1973.   2. Music—
Performance.   I. Title.
ML418.C4B6   780'.92'4   77-1444
ISBN 0-520-04032-5

The author and publisher are grateful to Novello & Company Ltd for
permission to reprint musical examples from the Elgar Cello Concerto,
and to E. P. Dutton & Co., Inc. and Hutchinson & Co. Ltd for
permission to quote extracts from *Conversations with Casals* by José Maria
Corredor. Copyright © 1956 by E. P. Dutton & Co., Inc.

PRINTED IN GREAT BRITAIN

CONTENTS

ILLUSTRATIONS

The musical examples have been drawn by Malcolm Lipkin.

I will say only elemental things, nothing com-
plicated – as everything ought to be, beginning
with life. But you must know that the simplest
things are the ones that count.

Pablo Casals

INTRODUCTION

by

PAUL TORTELIER

> the communication
> Of the dead is tongued with fire beyond the language of the living.
> T. S. ELIOT

It takes as much audacity as faith to write such a book as this. David Blum has lacked neither of these qualities and has thus succeeded in achieving the impossible. There is no page, indeed, in which those who knew Casals do not feel his presence or hear his voice; there is nothing that is not perfectly true. In summary, it is at one and the same time a film of the rehearsals, a detailed and minute analysis of the technique of interpretation (elucidated by means of clearly illustrated musical quotations), a commentary structured in such a manner that the thoughts of Casals are transmitted without loss of continuity in all their richness, strength and luminous simplicity. Finally, there is no tendency towards any sort of dogmatism, but on the contrary the demonstration that the art of Casals, elaborate as it may seem on close analysis, was never separated from the warmth of the soul and the heart, and always retained the spontaneous character of improvisation.

Pablo Casals, the greatest cellist of all time, owed the superiority of his interpretations to the quality of his convictions resulting from an exceptional musical intuition, based upon a broad knowledge and ever-strengthened by the sacred fire of exaltation.

'We must have exaltation,' Casals told the musicians around him – this, in reference to variations (exaltation of a theme), to trills (exaltation of a note), in fact, in regard to everything. As he would say: 'If there is no exaltation it is not good.' And the fire of exaltation in which he forged his convictions was fed by the constant wonder emanating from his contemplation of nature.

If well understood, the teaching of Casals may offer much, not only to those concerned with the interpretation of music, but also to composers who, when entering into the depth of Casals' thinking, will become aware of the infinite variety of nature and will rediscover at the same time their innate originality.

Returning to the interpreter, let it not be forgotten that real musical feeling, through which one can find the appropriate character of a given page, can only truly come from *within*. It would be a mistake to hope that it is possible to recreate the works of the great masters in all their beauty and truth by a merely theoretical application of Casals' principles. It seems that in the realm of musical creation and recreation, more are being called and fewer chosen. To remedy this situation, one needs to climb beyond the dangerous slope of mere facility and of quick recompense so contrary to art.[1] Young musicians must honour again the study of musical composition, following the example of the great interpreters of the past, not excluding Casals who, in fact, devoted time to composition all of his life.

May David Blum's work inspire the musical reader to draw strength again from nature, as did Beethoven and Schubert whenever they had the possibility, or to contemplate some Mount Canigou as Casals often did at sunrise. Then one's interpretations will be living and authentic because they will spring from deep sources, as with Casals, who, when once asked, 'How do you count here, Maestro?' answered: 'With my soul.'

[1] 'A work of art is never completed; it is only abandoned.' – Paul Valéry

FOREWORD
by
ANTONY HOPKINS

'TO be a legend in one's lifetime . . .' The phrase has become a cliché, debased by the ease with which the media today can create legends for a public ever hungry for new idols to worship. Yet such legendary figures do exist and have existed, figures whose stature is more enduring than that of the television interviewer, the newspaper columnist or the pop star. The true creators, writers, painters, sculptors and composers are ultimately judged by the value posterity places upon their work; thus the Work is in the long run more important than its Maker. Tastes may change; the critical esteem in which a composer is held may decline over a couple of decades, as it has with Sibelius, or be enhanced as it has with Janáček. The music lives on, renewing its vitality through performance. But what of the performer? Is his contribution to music too evanescent to be preserved? Recordings today have reached a sufficient perfection for us to be able to convince ourselves that 'legendary' performances of *our* time can now be captured for generations to come, as though by some miracle we were able to hear the actual sound of Liszt or Chopin across the gulf of years. Already we may feel a sense of awe as we listen to records (or pianola rolls) of Busoni, Godowsky, Kreisler or Chaliapin. The machine conjures up the long-dead sounds, but though we may marvel at the performance itself or at the technology that makes its resurrection possible, it remains a performance of the dead, and as we listen, our room is filled with their spectral presence. Instinctively and unavoidably we measure them against the yardstick of our contemporary giants, and because the latter are still with us, because they will play or sing for us again next week, next year, they have the power to put the ghosts in their place, to make them truly passé.

I only heard Casals once. Of course one says it was unforgettable, and so, in a way, it was. As long as I live I shall remember the sight of that homely almost dumpy little figure, more like a village organist than an internationally renowned soloist; as long as I live I shall remember the atmosphere he created around him, the uncanny hush as six thousand or more people in the Albert Hall seemed to hold their breath for the entire duration of the Bach sarabande he played as an encore. But can I truly say it was unforgettable? Do I remember every nuance, every bow-change, every accent? In all honesty I must say No. Say to me 'Listen to the records then', and I will reply that it is not enough. I could listen a thousand times and since each repetition would be identical so would the marvellous spontaneity of his interpretation seem to diminish. Gradually the machine would take over and that treasured visual memory of an actual occasion might even grow less vivid. Casals would cease to be the 'legend in his lifetime' and become a legend in his death, and the taint of death would lie upon him as he joined those other ghosts I have mentioned.

And so we come to the purpose of this book. Two years ago I spent a happy day in Geneva at the delightful home of David Blum. The conversation turned to Casals and such was David's enthusiasm as he spoke of him that I half expected that never-forgotten figure to walk in from the garden, take out his cello and play for us. Casals was no longer in a box of discs or imprisoned between the plastic covers of a record-sleeve. He was there, alive again, speaking through another's voice it's true, but nearer to me than he had ever been in life. 'Was there a place for a book about Casals,' David asked me, 'a book for musicians, detailed enough to go into the fundamental aspects of his art?' My answer was an emphatic Yes, since here I felt was a man whose devotion to Casals was such as to ensure a fidelity to truth – musical truth. Not being a string-player myself I might easily fall into the trap of saying that the book is not for me; to do so would be as foolish as it would have been to have turned Casals away from my door had he miraculously appeared there. In these pages there is something more important than memories of Casals, reminders of performances, annotations to recordings. Here is the means whereby that 'legend in his lifetime' may be kept alive so that every young musician may feel Casals in spirit standing by his side, exhorting, cajoling, teaching.

There have been other examples of such books; Johnson had his Boswell, Stravinsky his Robert Craft; yet there is a danger that if the disciple's notebook is too readily in evidence, the master may become too self-consciously aware of posterity. David Blum had his notebook to hand but he never forced himself upon Casals as a chronicler; he never even planned to write a book at the time. He simply wanted to treasure for his own use everything that he could gather of Casals' experience and wisdom. Only an intellectual miser would want to keep such riches to himself; it is our good fortune that this quiet observer has chosen to share this wealth with us so that we too may come under the spell of Pablo Casals and know him as a musician and teacher supreme.

Belgrade, June 1976

PREFACE

'IMAGINE!' Pablo Casals once said. 'They call me a great cellist. I am not a cellist; I am a musician. That is much more important.'

During the last decades of his life, Casals rarely appeared as a soloist; he devoted himself principally to conducting and teaching, passing on the depth and scope of a knowledge and understanding culled over a lifetime dedicated to the art of interpretation. He repeatedly stressed certain fundamental concepts which he sometimes called 'laws of music' or 'laws of nature' – concepts which he considered to be essential elements of meaningful interpretation and applicable to all forms of musical expression. My purpose in writing this book is to provide a study of these principles and, by giving selected examples from the repertoire, to draw a portrait of Casals the interpreter at work. Thus this book is not a biography, although the luminous strength of personality which so animated Casals and replenished his art cannot be entirely excluded from its pages; nor is it a manual for cellists, although it does incorporate the basic features of Casals' teaching in regard to string playing. It is an attempt to record in print the oral tradition of Casals' teaching of interpretation, to preserve this heritage for a new generation of musicians to whom he is now a legend.

Casals would sometimes refer to the innovations in technique which he had introduced – ideas which revolutionized cello playing in the twentieth century. However, he did not consider his musical concepts to be innovations. He was, in fact, in the historical mainstream of great interpreters. Casals' teaching shares much in common with the writings of C. P. E. Bach, Quantz, the Mozarts, father and son, Czerny's account of Beethoven's

playing, Liszt's description of Chopin's performance, the treatises
of Wagner. If Casals' ideas sometimes seemed startlingly new, it
was, as he pointed out, because 'the old natural rules have been
forgotten'.

While 'Casals the cellist' is a household expression, some
words may be in order about Casals, the conductor. Conducting
was for him not an occasional avocation as it has often been for
many famous instrumentalists. 'If I have been happy scratching
away at my cello,' he once wrote to Julius Röntgen, 'how shall I
feel when I can possess the greatest of all instruments – the
orchestra?' His conducting career, which began with the
Lamoureux Orchestra in 1908, extended over sixty-five years. In
1920 he founded the Orquestra Pau Casals in Barcelona, which
he conducted until the outbreak of the Spanish civil war. Sir
Adrian Boult, who attended Casals' rehearsals in 1923, comments, '. . . the rehearsals were really lessons . . . every member
of the orchestra was made to feel the passage himself in its inevitable relation to the expression of the moment and the style of
the whole work. . . . We all know Casals' playing of the classics.
Casals, the conductor, is no less great an artist.' During this
period, Casals also made frequent appearances as guest conductor
with such ensembles as the London Symphony Orchestra and the
Vienna Philharmonic. From 1950, his principle form of public
performance was in the capacity of conductor, whether at the
Prades or Marlboro Festivals or with the Festival Casals Orchestra
of Puerto Rico, an ensemble drawn from among the finest of
America's musicians, many first-desk players in major orchestras
taking secondary positions for the privilege of playing under his
direction. At no time did Casals communicate his ideas about
music more clearly or eloquently than when rehearsing an
orchestra. For this reason I have devoted much space to this
aspect of his music-making. The rehearsals in question, unless
otherwise stated, took place when he was conducting the Festival
Casals or Marlboro Festival orchestras.

In planning the format of this book I have divided the material
under chapter headings which are, I believe, representative of the

main aspects of Casals' teaching. Music being what it is, much of
the material is interrelated, and some overlapping is unavoidable.
To cite but one instance, the principles of clarity of articulation,
as set out in Chapter III, are closely related to string technique,
discussed in Chapter V. The final chapter, 'A Casals Rehearsal:
The Pastoral Symphony', provides an example of how the
various elements of interpretation, which are dealt with individually during the course of the book, join together in performance.

The musical examples are taken in nearly equal proportion
from among the cello and orchestral works which Casals taught
and performed. If, in writing this book, I have been obliged to
select only a limited number of musical quotations which I
thought would best exemplify the text, the reader is not so
bound. This book could serve no better purpose than to stimulate
the reader to discover for himself, among the vast repertoire of
great music, the way in which Casals' principles may find
extensive application. When, in the progress of the text, a piece
of music is examined in a new context, I have occasionally
repeated an example rather than impose a frequent need for cross-
referencing. Since not every music lover is well versed in the C
clefs, the musical examples are quoted in the G or F clef; (cellists
will, I hope, forgive me). The music of transposing instruments
has been written at actual pitch.

Casals' interpretative indications are contained within curved
brackets that they may be distinguished from composers' markings, which remain unbracketed. Generally, where Casals' indications elaborate upon those of the printed score, I have left the
two sets of markings standing side by side. The insertion of the
composers' markings has presented certain problems, since unani-
mity is often lacking among the various sources. Where possible,
I have consulted *Urtext* editions. (One notable exception is the
Boccherini B♭ major Concerto which Casals played in the
Grützmacher edition – the only one available during the first
part of this century, and which, despite the publication of an
authentic score, is still popular today among cellists.) With

Casals' indications other difficulties arise. There is, in any case, the general problem posed when one attempts to translate a living re-creation into signs and symbols. Furthermore, Casals' interpretations were not set in an inflexible mould; bowings and fingerings were frequently changed; expressive inflections were subject to subtle variation. To the extent that an imperfect system of notation permits, I have endeavoured to indicate Casals' interpretation as it was at a given point in time. The reader should take the bracketed markings to be butterflies observed for a moment while on the wing – not when pinned down in the lepidopterist's case.

The great majority of Casals' statements quoted in this book were originally spoken in English; his use of this language, while sometimes imperfect, was always expressive and compelling. Only in those few places where I felt that his grammatical usage left his meaning unclear have I slightly modified the syntax. The epigraph placed below each chapter title is quoted from Casals.

Although I began to write this book in 1975 it was, in a sense, born twenty-two years previously when, as a student, I first visited Prades. My notes were taken at rehearsals and master classes in Prades, Zermatt, San Juan, Marlboro, the University of California, in private discussions with Casals and at chamber music rehearsals at his home. But this has been for me more than 'note-taking'. Casals brought a love and dedication to every phrase he played; he transmitted an aura of tangible joy in his music-making which touched one not only at a cerebral level. One cannot write of these things in a spirit of abstraction and I make no apology if, in setting down these recollections, I have not withheld my own enthusiasm. However, it goes without saying that the information presented about Casals' teaching is recorded as faithfully and accurately as possible.

As with all great artists, Casals' approach to a given work could be highly individual. Obviously there will be more than one way to interpret any piece. However, it is the aim of this book to set forth Casals' ideas as clearly as possible, and it is beyond its province to discourse extensively upon alternative ways of teaching and performing.

What Casals left to us was not a doctrinaire system but an open door to our own experience. The strength of his spirit worked not to confine but to liberate; he guided a younger generation not towards a rigid copying of his ways, but towards an enriched understanding of the art of interpretation. He showed us, through his example, how we might open a musical score even for the hundredth time and yet never lack courage – as Shelley expressed it – 'to feel that which we perceive, and to imagine that which we know'.

I wish to express my gratitude to Antony Hopkins without whose encouragement this book might never have been written; to Peter Gras for his discerning attention given to my literary effort; to Bernard Greenhouse for his invaluable musical advice; and to Emile Ellberger, Beaumont Glass and Geoffrey Sutton for their many helpful suggestions. Among others who have kindly provided counsel or assistance are Orlanda Brugnola, Isidore Cohen, Prof. Vincent Duckles, Clive Fairbairn, Sidney Harth, Michael Kennedy, Nathan Kroll, Aurora Natola-Ginastera, Menahem Pressler, Franz Walter and Wolfgang Zuckermann. The photographs of Casals teaching were taken by Perren-Barberini, Zermatt, and provided by Constant Cachin.

Finally, I wish to thank Mary Worthington of Heinemann Educational Books for patiently seeing this volume through every editorial stage; and my wife – a musician in her own right and also a friend to Casals – for giving this work the benefit of her perceptive criticism.

Vandœuvres,   DAVID BLUM
Switzerland 1976

NOTE: the English terms 'minim', 'crotchet', 'quaver', 'semi-quaver' and 'demisemiquaver' are equivalent to the American 'half note', 'quarter note', 'eighth note', 'sixteenth note' and 'thirty-second note' respectively; while 'semitone' and 'tone' correspond to 'half step' and 'whole step' (or 'whole tone').

CHAPTER I

THE FIRST PRINCIPLE

Technique, wonderful sound . . . all of this is sometimes astonishing –
but it is not enough.

'As Western students of Oriental culture have discovered, the
First Principle does not lend itself to precise translation,'
said my Chinese friend, an art historian. 'It is something definite,
yet it is indescribable. It is how you feel when you enter a room
and sense that everything in it is somehow harmonious;
you know that you are at peace there. It is how your life
suddenly seems to change when you fall in love. It is the way in
which your spirit comes into subtle accord with the movement of
life around you; at the same time it is an experience within yourself – at the very centre. It is active and passive, embracing and
releasing; it is a profound sense of *being*.'

We were discussing *ch'i-yün*, the first of the Six Principles set
down by the art critic Hseih Ho in the fifth century A.D. in what
is thought to be the earliest document stating the fundamental
canons of Chinese painting. It was maintained that in order to
become a master, the artist must prove himself in the following
skills: vitality of brushstroke, accuracy in portrayal, versatility in
colouring, care in arrangement of composition, transmission of
tradition through copying the works of earlier masters. But the
foremost task lay in the fulfilment of the First Principle, which
has sometimes been defined as 'breath-resonance life-motion'.
For only by coming into harmony with the vital cosmic spirit or
breath could the painter convey through the movement of his
brush the mysterious vitality of life itself.

I

'The other five principles may be acquired through study and perseverance,' said my friend, 'but *ch'i-yün* comes from within. It develops in the silence of the soul.'

I recall one morning when Casals rehearsed Wagner's 'Siegfried Idyll' – the 'symphonic birthday greeting to his Cosima from her Richard', written in commemoration of their son's birth. After the opening bars had been played very beautifully, Casals stopped the orchestra, closed his eyes, and quietly clasped his hands together. For a long moment he became quite still, absorbed in contemplation. His transfigured expression reflected a oneness with the spirit from which this music is born: infinite devotion, profoundest love. Then, without a single word, he indicated that the orchestra should begin again. Aware or not of how or why they had been moved, the musicians brought to their playing a more inward quality of feeling, drawn from a source of deep tenderness; and from this source the entire work sang as if shimmering from a golden mirror. Although Casals paused to rehearse points of detail, the continuity of feeling remained unbroken. The long transitional passage has never been more delicately woven: the trills were suspended like threads of magic light; there was alchemy in the air. The woodwind and strings, in turn, gave gentle invocation to the new theme:

Ex. I

'Although it is pianissimo,' Casals said, 'every note must sing!' The pulse quickened; the music flowed ardently – inevitably –

towards its climax. At the entrance of the horn call Casals stopped, desperate for words; finally he blurted out: '*Joy*! It is the announcement of the birth of his son. He is so happy!'

I have never heard anyone so utterly express the meaning of a given word as did Casals. When he said 'joy' . . . 'lovely' . . . 'tender' . . . each word conveyed a resonance of feeling, as did his playing of a phrase by Bach. No person meeting Casals for the first time would come away unmoved – if not unshaken – by these simple words which had not lost their connection with their origin in spirit. Who else could risk saying 'Be sincere' and strike to the heart's core?

This sense of wonder, of touching upon an original experience, was the essence of Casals' art; the manner in which this wonder was crystallized into supreme music-making was the secret of his greatness.

Far from the bliss of the 'Siegfried Idyll' is the Schumann Cello Concerto, a work of feverish unrest and dark foreboding. Clara Schumann recounts the harrowing scene in which her husband, having been tormented by the alternating visitations of angels and demons, began correcting his Cello Concerto, 'hoping that this would deliver him from the perpetual sound of the voices'. In keeping with his usual teaching procedure Casals first asked his student to play through a large section of this work, after which he made appropriate comments about intonation, improved fingering and other pertinent matter. As always, his explanations were brief and directly to the point. Casals then began to play, taking the student through the piece phrase by phrase. As he did so, he became increasingly immersed in the emotional atmosphere of the work. 'Pain, pain . . .' he called out. 'All is pain – the poor man!' In one passage Casals' bow slashed upon the string and then forged a hair-raising crescendo, culminating in a sforzando that had the intensity of a shriek; the answering phrase came as an inconsolable lament:

Ex. 2

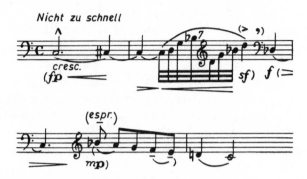

Within the space of a few minutes the lesson had imperceptibly transformed itself from a fascinating account of cello playing into a uniquely moving human experience. 'Doloroso . . . doloroso!' Casals' voice rose almost in a wail. 'Everything in this concerto is espressivo.'

For Casals, the formulation of feeling and the interpretation of music emanated from a single source and flowed together in a single stream. Notes which stood apart from this stream were 'cold – without meaning'.

'Announce the hero!' he exclaimed, when a student was about to begin the Dvořák Concerto. This was no mere rhetoric. Dvořák's work was, to Casals, an heroic drama, passing through every vicissitude of expression. The tale of Casals' refusal to perform the concerto with a conductor who disparaged it is no myth but a true instance of his deep involvement. Towards the end of the last movement where the cello subsides in a long diminuendo, Casals conceived the moment of final expiration as portraying 'the death of the hero'.

Ex. 3

The Saint-Saëns Cello Concerto in A minor presented another kind of drama. Casals reminisced: 'This work is an old friend of mine; I played it with Saint-Saëns when I was twelve.[1] Saint-Saëns explained to me that this concerto was inspired by the Pastoral Symphony of Beethoven. It opens with a storm; then come moments of calm.'

'Here, where the theme comes in D major, we begin to see some blue in the sky':

Ex. 4

'And, as in Beethoven, there is a peasants' dance; here we must play lightly and simply – with very little vibrato':

Ex. 5

Not all his descriptions were so precise. Sometimes no more than a few words, barely spoken above a whisper, would give a hint of the inner vision which illuminated the re-creative process.

'As in a dream,' he said, when rehearsing a passage from the slow movement of Beethoven's Fourth Symphony:

[1] At which time the composer called Casals' performance the finest he had ever heard.

Ex. 6

At the beginning of the third movement of Beethoven's D major Cello Sonata:

Ex. 7

he commented, 'These are not notes – they are only a first impression; they seem to say "what comes now?" – mystery, mystery . . .'

Casals did not consider the rococo style, as found for instance in works of Haydn and Boccherini, to be an archaic remnant of the past. 'We must play this music with all its grace – it is so free, fresh and lovely. Not one note dry!' In the first movement of the Haydn D major Concerto, he assigned leading operatic roles: here, in the low register, the cello was to sing 'like a basso cantante'; there, in the upper register, 'with the elegance of a prima donna'. The very highest notes were formed into enchanting arabesques: 'Always something lovely, always singing . . .'

But Casals well understood that the world of the rococo was but one side of Haydn's art. His interpretations brought to vivid realization the contrasts of dark and light in the Symphony No. 95, the interplay of charm and rusticity in the 'Surprise'

Symphony, the romantic longing in the Adagio from the
'Farewell' Symphony. When reading through the score of the
'Mourning' Symphony (No. 44) he exclaimed to me: 'Haydn
could do anything!'

Some musicians would restrict and categorize the degree of expression which may be brought to the performance of music of
the 'classical' period. Casals was not the person to withhold the
First Principle from any musical interpretation. He did not
undervalue the depth of feeling with which our ancestors
experienced the music that they composed and performed. Those
living in the eighteenth century did not regard their art as
'classical'; it was a living event.

'Would you like to know how I have expressed and even indicated the beating, loving heart?' wrote Mozart. 'By two violins
playing in octaves . . . . You feel the trembling – the faltering –
you see how the throbbing breast begins to heave; this I have
indicated by a crescendo. You hear the whispering and the
sighing . . .'[1]

When Casals conducted Mozart's Symphony No. 40, the
mood of impassioned agitation spoke to us immediately. 'We
must not be afraid to give expression,' Casals exclaimed. 'There
are very few markings of course. Mozart knew all that was in the
piece. He was the composer; he was the one who suffered.' Where
the second subject comes in G minor (Ex. 8), Casals gave voice to
the feeling inherent in the phrase with but a single word: 'Grief!'
– indicating with his baton that the initial note should come like
a heartwound. The descending chromatic notes were allowed
time to speak their sorrow. In the fifth bar came a new wave of
expression, more intensive than the first. At the conclusion of
each phrase there arose lesser waves of unstilled anguish:

[1] In this, Mozart showed himself to be a true son to his father, for Leopold once
wrote: 'It is as clear as sunlight that every effort must be made to put the player in the
mood which reigns in the piece itself, in order thereby to penetrate the souls of the
listeners and to excite their emotions.'

Ex. 8

When, in the coda, the first subject is passed from one instrumental group to another, Casals urged that the phrases be sung with fervent intensity: 'I hear only notes – no despair!'

Ex. 9

Casals' gestures when conducting were never rigid or mechanical; they went with the musical phrase and had a natural line of beauty which no school of conducting can teach. He used a score, in his advanced years sat on a chair, and approached the conductor's art with true simplicity. He would often begin a rehearsal by working in detail; a quarter of an hour could be devoted to two or three phrases. His aim exceeded technical perfection; it was to reveal the power of life inherent in music. For example, the opening bars of Bach's First Orchestral Suite are easy to play, but, as Casals pointed out, they can just as easily sound 'heavy and monotonous'. Rehearsing with care that each semiquaver be given dynamic gradation, he shaped a lyric contour. 'Every note has to have a different sonority,' he insisted; 'it is a song.'

Ex. 10

Ouverture

The phrase was gone over repeatedly, each time gaining in eloquence and vitality. Finally Casals said, 'Something like that' (how often were these words heard from him!), meaning that the goal, though elusive, had been touched upon. Now, stopping less often, he gave the orchestra rein to play through longer sections, the musicians, already brought to a high pitch of awareness and sensibility, responding to his every indication of expression.

Casals' rehearsals were challenging, creative experiences for all present. Having played as principal cellist under both Toscanini and Casals, Frank Miller comments: 'Casals, such a great musician both as cellist and conductor, would seek out the essential meaning of a work as did Toscanini, but each in his own way, for they were such different personalities. Like Toscanini, Casals tolerated nothing less than the complete revelation of the music's heart and soul and inspired the profoundest respect from the musicians who played under his direction.'

Casals communicated an unreserved joy in the process of music-making. As a cellist he knew full well that one must sometimes take risks to be expressive. To encourage the horns to produce an uninhibited crescendo in a difficult passage from the third movement of Beethoven's 'Eroica', he said: 'Let us make the crescendo right to the end of the phrase. Play without fear. If the note doesn't come out, you're welcome all the same.'

Ex. 11

The note did come out, and with rousing vigour.

In the Andante con moto from Mozart's Symphony No. 39, at the arrival of the following forte passage:

Ex. 12

Casals called out, 'Full – full!' He rose from his chair and spread out his arms in a great gesture of openness and acceptance, saying, 'Like this – like this!' The musicians responded with playing of luminous warmth. Their capacity for expression had suddenly been enlarged by Casals' fidelity to the voice of his own feeling.

A remark that Casals often made, and which typified him as man and musician, was 'play frankly'. He would apply these words to the end of a phrase which had to convey a sense of completeness:

Ex. 13 Beethoven: *Symphony No. 4*, 2nd mvt.

to semiquavers which should be stated directly and simply:

Ex. 14 Dvořák: *Cello Concerto*, 2nd mvt.

to the forte chord which follows each lyrical phrase at the opening of the Andante cantabile from Mozart's 'Jupiter' Symphony:

Ex. 15

To 'play frankly' is not to eschew subtlety and refinement. It is to play, where the music so demands, forthrightly, without sentimentality; to state what we feel unashamedly and unhesitatingly.

How can one do justice in words to the range of Casals' expression? No musician could evoke more sense of power from an instrument or declaim a passage with more intensity. His performance of the Finale of Brahms' E minor Cello Sonata was a

titanic experience; relentless in its drive, the quavers fell like hail-
stones. 'Give all your strength,' he said, when teaching the
following passage from the first movement of Beethoven's D
major Sonata:

Ex. 16

'Break your cello! It is better to have character in what you play
than to have a beautiful sound.'

It was a different Casals teaching the second movement of the
Lalo Concerto:

Ex. 17

'Lovely, lovely — there is nothing of violence here. It is so
elegant, so Spanish. With grace — beautiful, poetic! I haven't
played that for thirty-five years at least, and I still remember.'[1]

Casals brought to the Elgar Concerto an intensity of feeling
and wealth of inflection which had not hitherto been associated
with that work. Neville Cardus describes Casals' performance:
'. . . the question of the evening was whether the so-called
"Englishness" of Elgar would elude him . . . let it emphatically

[1] It was with this work that Casals made his début in Paris on 12 November 1899.

be said that the work has never before sounded so eloquent, so beautifully and so finely composed as now . . ... The slow movement put some of us for a while under an obligation not to breathe. The falling sequences of the coda, one of the most heartfelt in existence and one of the most original in "shape", were as though sorrow and sympathy stood before us wringing their hands.' Some critics complained that Casals' approach lacked a certain 'austerity'; it was too 'foreign' (i.e. emotional). Elgar had thought differently. He valued Casals' interpretation, he said, because Casals had made the concerto sound like 'such a big work'.

Such a big work – but Casals was such a small man, and a simple man. The music came not from histrionics, flourishes, excesses, but from the way it moved him in his inner life. Such was the richness of his soul that, on the one hand, his music touched the peasant earth with all its indomitable strength and exuberance; on the other, it held discourse with the sublime.

An indelible impression: Casals playing a slow movement of Bach, his eyes closed, his concentration removed from all daily anxieties and ambitions. He seems surrounded by a vast, unfathomable silence from which emerges the voice of his cello. He plays for himself and yet not only for himself; for each of us is, in his own way, alone with that voice, speaking to us in tones of inexpressible purity.

While the painters of ancient China agreed that the indispensable attribute of a great artist was his ability to convey the indefinable quality embodied in the First Principle, it was also understood that an artist will not succeed in expressing the First Principle until he has mastered each of the requisite skills. Form remains lifeless when not animated by spirit; yet, lacking knowledge and method, the energy of spirit will not be transmitted to the work of art.

In subsequent chapters we will look at the main features of Casals' teaching, the canons of his artistry, each of which is related to a unifying goal, that which the Chinese call *ch'i-yün*.

Casals once said: 'You will see where to make the vibrato, the crescendo, the diminuendo of the notes – all those things you have to have present, but present more in your feelings. Not present only here,' he said, as he tapped on his head, 'because it is not profound enough; but here' – and he drew his hand to his heart.

CHAPTER II

FINDING THE DESIGN

Remember that all music, in general, is a succession of rainbows.

A first encounter is often the most memorable. The year was
1953; the setting: the venerable abbey of St-Michel-de-
Cuxa in the foothills of the Pyrenees; the work: Mozart's
Symphony No. 39 in E♭ major. On that occasion Casals was
rehearsing the second movement.

At the beginning of the principal theme, Mozart has provided
the indication *piano*; there is no change in dynamic marking for
twenty-nine bars. I had heard this passage performed, even by
eminent conductors, with so little dynamic nuance as to verge
upon the monotonous, and by virtue of these interpretations I felt
the theme somehow to fall short of being truly beautiful and
deeply stirring. I wanted to be moved by it more than I actually
was; the melody remained for me something of an enigma. What
solution might Casals offer, I wondered.

'Although only piano is written,' he said, 'we must follow the
line of the music; we must find the design!' He began to
conduct.

The brief opening phrase was indeed played piano, nobly and
simply, falling away at the end in diminuendo. He then indicated that the ascending line should develop in a gradual
crescendo, the demisemiquavers providing a life-communicating
power of movement.[1] As the theme approached its summit,
Casals rose from his chair, greeting the climax with open arms,

[1] See Chapter IV on the vitality of dotted rhythms.

15

lingering with heartfelt tenderness on the crotchet before allowing it to expire like a sigh.

Ex. 18

Bars 5–8 were similarly transfigured into a flowing wave – a
wave which followed a natural urge towards its crest, attained
fulfilment and then subsided with ineffable loveliness.

This was the first music lesson I received from Casals and it
went through me like lightning. Although dynamic inflections
are not indicated in the score, Casals had allowed the intensity of
expression to evolve organically with the melodic curve. The
phrasing seemed inevitable, logical and perfectly natural. The
theme was revealed in all its splendour – classical in the beauty of
its proportions, romantic in its declaration of feeling.

It was not until some years later that I was to read Richard
Wagner's commentary upon Mozart interpretation with its
reference to this very theme.

Take Mozart's instrumental pieces ... two things are at once apparent: the melodies must be beautifully *sung*; yet there are very few
marks in the score to show *how* they are to be sung. It is well known
that Mozart wrote the scores of his symphonies hurriedly, in most
cases simply for the purpose of performance at some concert he was
about to give; on the other hand, it is also well known that he made
great demands upon the orchestra in the matter of expression. Obviously he trusted to his personal influence over the musicians. In the
orchestra parts it was thus sufficient to note the main tempo and

piano or forte for entire periods, since the master, who conducted the
rehearsals, could give spoken direction as to details, and, by singing
his themes, communicate the proper expression to the players . . . .
The traditions of such casual performances are completely lost. No
trace is preserved, except the scantily-marked scores. And these
classical relics of a once warmly vibrating work are now accepted,
with mistaken trust, as the sole guide towards a new living performance . . . . Let us examine a particular case – for example, the first
eight bars of the second movement of Mozart's celebrated
Symphony in E♭. Take this beautiful theme as it appears on paper,
with hardly any marks of expression – fancy it played smoothly and
complacently, as the score apparently has it – and compare the result
with the manner in which a true musician would feel and sing it!
How much of Mozart does the theme convey, if played, as in nine
cases out of ten it *is* played, in a perfectly colourless and lifeless way?
'Poor pen-and-paper music, without a shadow of soul or sense.'

'The manner in which a true musician would feel and sing it!'
Could a better description be found of Casals, the interpreter?
Lest it be thought that Wagner – and Casals – were viewing
Mozart through the spectacles of what is sometimes called nine-
teenth-century romanticism, let us take note of some commen-
taries on interpretation set down by composers living in the
eighteenth century.

Leopold Mozart:

Every care must be taken to find and to render the affect which
the composer wished to have brought out . . . . Indeed, one must
know how to change from soft to loud without directions and of
one's own accord, each at the right time; for this, in the familiar
language of painters, means *light* and *shade*.

Geminiani:

One of the principal Beauties of the Violin is the swelling or encreas-
ing and softening the Sound.

Quantz:

Good execution must be *diversified*. Light and shadow must be continuously interchanged. For in truth you will never move the listener
if you render all the notes at the same strength or the same weakness;
if you perform, so to speak, always in the same colour, or do not
know how to raise or moderate the tone at the proper time.

C. P. E. Bach:

Play from the soul, not like a trained bird![1]

Expressive inflection as an indispensable element in musical
performance, and the introduction of expressive markings into
musical scores, are historically two different matters.[2] The manuscript of the Elgar Cello Concerto is liberally marked with indications of dynamic nuance; that of a Bach solo cello suite
contains not a single one. Yet both these works confess secrets of
the heart; both abound in a subtlety and variety of inflection that
surpass by far the most fastidious of interpretative markings.

'Variety,' Casals would say, 'is a great word – in music as in
everything; variety is a law of nature. Good music has never
monotony. If it is monotonous it is our own fault if we don't play
it as it has to be played . . . . We must give to a melody its natural
life. When the simple things and natural rules that are forgotten
are put in the music – then the music comes out!'

These 'natural rules', which he conveyed time and again in his
teaching, were born of logic based upon intuition. They expressed
elemental truths often hidden from us by the familiarity

[1] 'All who have heard [C. P. E.] Bach play the clavichord must have been struck by
the endless nuances of shadow and light that he casts over his performance.' – C. F.
Cramer, *Magazin der Musik*; Hamburg 1783.

[2] Bernard Shaw, recounting that 'Oscar Wilde sent the MS of *An Ideal Husband* to
the Haymarket Theatre without taking the trouble to note the entrances and exits of
the persons on the stage', comments: 'There is no degree of carelessness that is not
credible to men who know that they will be present to explain matters when serious
work begins.'

engendered by habit and routine. They recalled to mind the kinship between music and the elemental forces around and within
us.

Nature is permeated with an unceasing ebb and flow, manifest
in the change of seasons, the alternation of day and night, the
movement of tides. Perpetual oscillation is at the core of
biological life – the beating of our hearts, the rhythm of our
breathing. Nor are these fluctuations restricted to physical
phenomena. Our thoughts, fantasies, emotions, dreams flow in
waves, expanding to varying points of culmination before subsiding. 'Nature never stays at one level,' Casals reflected; 'there is
a constant vibration.'

Music, too, partakes in this ebb and flow – in the interplay
between tonality and modulation, in the counter-poise of unity
and diversity which together comprise form. Within the large
structural spans there are smaller waves – expressive of melodic,
rhythmic and harmonic intensities – wherein is contained the
moment-to-moment life of music.

Casals has stated, 'Each note is like a link in a chain – important
in itself and also as a connection between what has been and what
will be.' When he played, these links became living art. Every
phrase was borne upon a movement of energy which flowed
from one note through the next, going towards a point or
coming from another, ever in flux, ever formulating a contour.
A fundamental aim of his teaching was to show how the interpreter may come to recognize the expressive implication of
each phrase, and how he can bring that expression to full realization by the use of dynamic variety, rhythmic flexibility, tone
colour, intonation. Of these, dynamic variety is perhaps the most
immediate and elemental way in which the performer may 'give
to a melody its natural life'.[1]

Let us look at the theme of the Adagio from Haydn's D major
Cello Concerto, observing the manner in which Casals revealed
its design by means of dynamic inflection:

[1] The other factors, mentioned above, will be dealt with in Chapters IV and V.

Ex. 19

Analysis of Casals' interpretation tells us the following:

The dynamic level does not remain constant; within the forte there is room for the nuances to evolve flexibly.

Repetitions bring about a subtle variance in intensity, whether in the reiteration of the same note (for example, the two E's in Bar 1) or the repetition of a phrase (Bar 2, which restates Bar 1 sequentially).

The dynamic inflections respond to the rise and fall in pitch.

The long notes (in Bars 5 and 6) increase in intensity, thereby contributing to the development of the overall line.

These life-giving nuances reflect certain basic concepts of phrasing which Casals often expressed in words – concepts which, while not automatically and thoughtlessly applied, have sufficient general validity to be included here as a selection of his guiding principles in interpretation.

If the design goes up we must give a little more tone; if it goes down, a little less tone. This does not mean that there are not exceptions; there are always exceptions. But this is the general rule. Don't be afraid; let us be natural.

Generally, a long note will mean crescendo or diminuendo . . . . We must know how much to give, depending on what the music does. The note has to say something; one must give form, expression, interest.

An immediate repetition should provide contrast – a little more forte or piano; a change of colour. Otherwise it is not music. Variety – the art consists in that!

And the principle which embraced all the others:

When we see piano, the composer means in the *range* of piano. The range of piano extends all the way to forte and the range of forte extends all the way to piano. One has to follow the line of the music. If it goes up you have to give more, despite the piano. Otherwise it is something that is not free – not what the music intends.

In Casals' hands, these 'simple things', these 'natural rules' were like the trusted tools of an old wood-carver who knew well their formative power. Let us observe Casals at work with these tools, delineating those timeless features which stir within us an immediate sense of recognition.

We will begin by considering the first of the concepts stated above: namely, the manner in which dynamic inflection gives expressive form to the melodic curve. As in all essential things, Casals expressed himself simply. 'Remember,' he said, 'that all music, in general, is a succession of *rainbows*.' He demonstrated this by playing a passage from Bach's First Cello Suite:
'Here is a rainbow':   'And here, another':

Ex. 20a   Ex. 20b

'And now, a longer rainbow':

Ex. 20c

'Rainbows . . . rainbows; nearly all the music is like that. If one only makes this observation it is already a guide.'

It will be noted that each of these rainbows is different, the second being of lesser dynamic intensity than the first, while the third is lifted over an extended span. The rainbow arcs which Casals traced in music were imbued with the secret of proportion. They expressed the innate architecture of the phrase, be it the gradually unfolding melody which begins Bach's Second Cello Suite:

Ex. 21

the noble cantilena of Beethoven's A major Sonata:

Ex. 22

or the radiant curve of the singing line in Mozart's 'Linz' Symphony:

Ex. 23

In the above example the diminuendo in Bar 6 provides a softer starting point for the beginning of the rainbow. This momentary easing of intensity gives the interpreter greater freedom to mould dynamic nuances within the phrase without exceeding the just proportions of the overall level of volume. 'In this way,' Casals would say, 'the diminuendo gives economy to the crescendo that follows.'

We see a similar pattern of tension and relaxation within the following theme from the first movement of Schumann's Fourth Symphony:

Ex. 24

Casals asked the first violins to begin with singing tone in mezzo piano, make a diminuendo with the descending line, and then rise in a crescendo to the high D – which crowns the phrase even though it comes at a rhythmically weak point of the bar. Shaped in this way, the theme was freed from the dictates of the bar line; within these ten notes was contained a world of passion. The accompanying figure in the second violins was to be brought into prominence: 'Here is the anguish!' Casals cried out.

In his urge to *complete* a phrase, to soar through its higher notes, Casals' feeling for melody was closely allied to vocal art. How often would he ask his students to translate the natural flow of song into their bows: 'Sing at the top of the phrase!'

Ex. 25   Schumann: *Cello Concerto*, 3rd mvt.

There was, in fact, a remarkable similarity between Casals'
teaching of interpretation and that of Lotte Lehmann, not only in
the way in which these two great artists brought into being the
spiritual atmosphere of a musical composition, but in terms of
their fundamental approach to phrasing. In her book *More than
Singing*, Lotte Lehmann has written:

> It almost seems superfluous to say: never forget that a phrase must
> always have a main word and with it a musical high point. Yet it is
> incredible how often this elementary and self-evident fact is
> neglected . . . . Again and again I am astonished anew by a lack of
> musical feeling for the essential nature of the phrase . . . . Singing
> should never be just a straight going ahead, it should have a sweep-
> ing flow, it should glide in soft rhythmical waves which follow one
> another harmoniously.

While Casals normally counselled his students that 'when the
notes go up there is a natural crescendo', he would add, 'your intuition will tell you when the exceptions occur.' A change of
timbre or a rhythmic elongation was often the preferred means of
communicating the desired nuance. For instance, when playing
the opening theme of the Brahms E minor Sonata, Casals would
arrive at the high point (G) with a sudden understatement; the
note was imbued with a sense of mystery.

Ex. 26

In the closing theme of the first movement of Beethoven's Cello Sonata in F major, the composer has placed a sforzando on the D preceding the highest note (F). Casals observed this sforzando and then brought attention to the F by a subtle rhythmic elongation.[1]

Ex. 27

Some themes begin on the note of uppermost pitch. Generally in such cases (as in Exs. 28–30), Casals, with characteristic directness, would start at the high point of expression, bringing an immediate warmth to the first note. The specific quality of expression would be in keeping with the mood of the given work.

Ex. 28   Mozart: *Symphony No. 40*, 2nd mvt.

Ex. 29   Beethoven: *Symphony No. 4*, 2nd mvt.

[1] See Chapter IV: agogic accents.

Ex. 30   Schumann: '*Adagio and Allegro*', Op. 70

We have observed in the theme of the Adagio from the Haydn
D major Cello Concerto the value which Casals placed upon the
expressive capacity of long notes, those sustained links in the
chain of melodic evolution. Like a slow gesture in dance, a long
note must preserve the continuity of line; otherwise it will arrest
the sense of motion. When teaching the opening movement of
Bach's First Viola da Gamba Sonata, Casals commented, 'If the
long note stays on the same level it becomes monotonous. One is
waiting for something. Well, that *something* is to give colour to
that long note. If you do a little crescendo, then the interest continues; you will see how beautiful it is.'

Ex. 31

In Ex. 32 the crescendo within the long note provides the growing weight which supports the melodic arch. Lacking this, we would have just another case of 'poor pen-and-paper music'.

Ex. 32   Bach: *Viola da Gamba Sonata No. 2*, 1st mvt.

A delicate crescendo over the sustained notes in Ex. 33 leads us to the summit of this most lyrical of phrases:

Ex. 33   Schumann: *Cello Concerto*, 1st mvt.

Casals brought to the principal subject of Wagner's 'Siegfried Idyll' a gentle, swaying motion. The long notes, coming in diminuendo, provided a gliding sense of release. The rising scale had the quality of an upbeat:

Ex. 34

The sustained note with which the cello enters in the slow movement of the Boccherini B♭ major Concerto was played with a curve of intensity which reached its peak at the bar line, after which it began to attenuate.

Ex. 35

'Do not forget,' Casals would say, 'that in piano there is a range of expression and sonority. Even if you play piano in general – give colour in that piano.'

Under certain circumstances, Casals pointed out, one note will contain a dual impulse of relaxation and subsequent renewal of tension, as in the opening movement of Mozart's Symphony No. 39.

Ex. 36

The A♮ first follows its natural tendency towards expiration; then, functioning as a suspension, it bridges over to the melodic figure in the next bar.

Again, a dual impulse comes about when the note of resolution following an appoggiatura (which has an inherent diminuendo) is succeeded by a higher note to which it must establish a melodic connection:

Ex. 37   Bach: *Viola da Gamba Sonata No. 2*, 3rd mvt.

Ex. 38   Schumann: *Cello Concerto*, 1st mvt.

We now come to the question of reiteration. Repetition in music – be it of a single note or of a phrase – is similar to repetition of words or phrases in speech. It is a natural feature of expressive communication that we vary the emphasis when we say the same thing more than once. Reiterating 'I love you' in a monotone will not get you very far. When, in the last act of *King Lear*, the despairing monarch addresses the lifeless body of Cordelia:

> Thou'lt come no more,
> Never, never, never, never, never!

the first thing an actor will instinctively realize is that he must vary the force of intensity from one word to the next. He will achieve repetition without duplication. 'It is a general rule that repeated notes or a repeated design must not be equal,' Casals would remind his students. 'Something has to be done. Otherwise you have monotony – and nothing is more monotonous than monotony!'

When considering repetitions of single notes, we must first determine whether they are moving towards a point of rhythmic strength or receding from it. For example, in the final movement of Bach's Third Gamba Sonata, the groups of reiterated quavers have the character of upbeats; Casals asked that they come each time in an impassioned crescendo: 'In those short notes we must give something!'

Ex. 39a

at Bar 95:

Ex. 39b

Conversely, the triplet quavers in the 'Siegfried Idyll' fall away, as it were, from the first beat of the bar. (The movement towards repose continues through the minim.)

Ex. 40

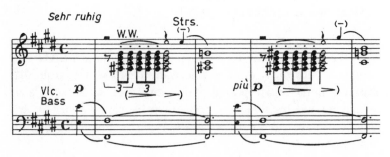

When rehearsing the woodwind in the second movement of Mozart's Symphony No. 39, Casals took care that each successive quaver should convey a sense of dynamic growth, while remaining within a tonal framework that would preserve the mood of tranquillity.

Ex. 41¹

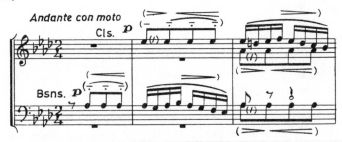

In the above example it will be noted that the first bassoon commences on the second quaver of the bar; each of the three quavers has an upbeat impulse. The clarinets and second bassoon, however, begin on the first quaver of the bar. This note, being the downbeat, subsides in diminuendo, bringing economy to the crescendo that follows.

The principle of ebb and flow is again evident in Casals' interpretation of the Andante from Mozart's Symphony No. 40; he brought to the reiterated quavers a living, contoured movement.¹

Ex. 42

¹ See Chapter III for a discussion of repeated notes with special reference to articulation.

No less does the 'law of diversity' apply to the repetition of phrases.

'If you say the same thing in the same way, it has no value,' Casals insisted when teaching the first movement of Brahms' E minor Sonata. 'The second time we must give more intensity.'

Ex. 43

Similarly, in the second movement of the Dvořák Concerto Casals would tell his students, 'As this phrase comes three times, try to have every time a little something else!'

Ex. 44

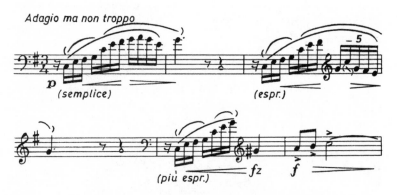

The reiterated passage in the first movement of the Haydn D major Concerto was varied in the most delightful way. Casals played the initial phrase in forte, with rhythmic vigour and rustic accents (the lower notes being performed as quavers). The repetition came in mezzo piano, cantabile (the lower notes omitted):

Ex. 45

In the second subject of the opening movement of Mendelssohn's 'Italian' Symphony, the initial two-bar phrase is repeated (in slightly modified form) at a lower pitch, after which it begins to rise sequentially. 'If we have the same sonority up and down it is not natural, not normal,' Casals commented. 'Let us give the natural variety. How lovely, how simple!'[1]

Ex. 46

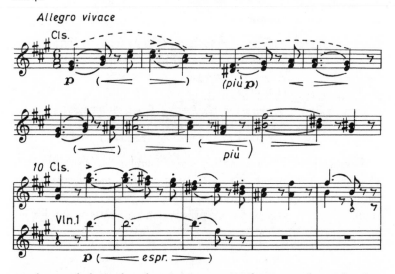

In the tenth bar, the clarinets arrive at their meridian; the first violins respond with a sustained high B. For Casals this note was a culmination of expression: 'Like a star!'

[1] Casals cautioned against exaggeration; an 'echo' effect is generally to be avoided 'because that would be out of proportion. What we do must always be in good taste.'

In Exs. 47 and 48, the immediate repetition of the phrase leads upwards in pitch. In each case Casals gave form to the melody by bringing its point of climax (+) into relief.

Ex. 47   Beethoven: *Symphony No. 2*, 2nd mvt.

Ex. 48   Beethoven: *Symphony No. 8*, 4th mvt.

The Andante from Bach's Second Gamba Sonata provides a characteristic example of Casals' way of building tension over a long melodic span by the contouring of individual phrases. In the theme itself he varied the (expressive) accentuation as follows:

Ex. 49a

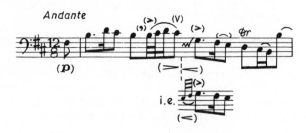

avoiding, in this way, the reiteration of a similar-sounding accent and clarifying the directional structure of the phrase. Later in the movement, where stanzas are built up through sequential repetition, each phrase retained, in miniature, its ebb and flow; yet each increased in intensity, contributing to the cumulative growth of the whole.

Ex. 49b

Textbooks define a sequence as repetitions of a melodic segment (with or without its harmony) at other levels, higher or lower. But they seldom mention that each segment, whether moving within a given key or engaged in modulation, expresses something different from its predecessor. While these repetitions may look alike to the eye, the subtle and changing relationships of tones and semitones within the structure of a scale produce continuous variations to the discerning ear. Casals, not insensitive to this fact, brought to each sequence delicate modifications of colour and intensity.

The 9/8 theme from the first movement of the Elgar Cello Concerto begins at a point near its melodic crest, and then unfolds in a gradually descending sequence. Casals communicated immediately the theme's heartrending quality; he brought to the very first note an eloquent, poignant vibrancy and drew attention to the highest note by means of a barely perceptible rubato. 'This melody,' he would say, 'must descend like a leaf which falls from a tree in the autumn – never a direct descent, but a series of gently cascading movements...'

Ex. 50

Again constructed of sequential elements, the main subject of the first movement of Schumann's Fourth Symphony expresses its despair turbulently, fiercely. The composer has left only two dynamic markings: a forte in the first bar and a fortissimo in the eleventh bar. In giving inflection to the melodic rise and fall, Casals in no way reduced the effectiveness of the forte. On the contrary, the relentless building up of tension in phrase after phrase had an overwhelming emotional impact.

Ex. 51

It was highly characteristic of Casals to bring a melody to life from within by giving individual contour to the various segments of which it is comprised.

In the introductory Adagio from Beethoven's Fourth Symphony the melodic line of the strings is normally sustained at an unvarying dynamic level, despite the extremely slow tempo. Casals' phrasing relieved any sense of monotony by drawing attention to the expressive fall of the motif of a descending third.

Ex. 52

In the following passage from the Finale of the same work, each of the first two bars was stressed as an entity in itself, resounding anew with vivacious lilt.

Ex. 53

Casals described the Trio from Beethoven's Eighth Symphony as 'a wonderful barcarolle!' Conducting in one flowing beat per bar, swaying slowly from side to side, he indicated to the horns a gentle break between the first and the second bars.

Ex. 54

When Casals conducted this work with the Vienna Philharmonic in 1927, the first horn player, unwilling to accept any interpretation which broke with tradition, walked out during the rehearsal. Although the gentleman in question reappeared for the concert and performed the passage in the manner requested, the incident typified for Casals the 'routine which can play havoc even with the best orchestra in the world'.

In the impassioned second subject of the opening movement of Brahms' E minor Cello Sonata, Casals asked that the third and fourth bars not be conceived as a single phrase unit. There was to be a 'slight separation', the fourth bar coming with feverishly renewed intensity.

Ex. 55

In the closing theme, where the motif first heard in minor comes again in major, Casals commented, 'You have to make a division; it says another thing.'[1]

Ex. 56

When Casals rehearsed the opening theme of Mozart's Symphony No. 40, he first drew attention to the character of the prime motif – the appoggiatura which contains a 'natural diminuendo':  ; the reiterations of this motif were to come with increased dynamic strength. Each four-bar phrase described an arc, the second (a tone lower in pitch) reaching a slightly lesser point of intensity.

Ex. 57a

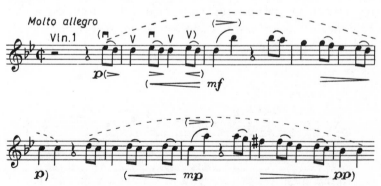

[1] He also stressed the importance of 'taking a breath' before the D♯ in the fifth bar of the first subject (see Ex 26).

The ensuing phrases developed with reinforced urgency, culminating in the high C of the woodwind, a note usually understated in performance but to which Casals granted its full expressive value.

Ex. 57b

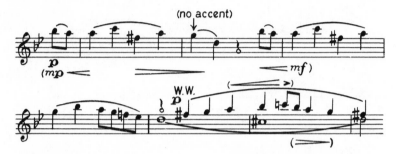

Conductors usually impose an uninterrupted legato upon the allegro subject from Mozart's Symphony No. 39, in quest of ideal beauty. Casals, too, conceived this theme lyrically, but *within* the lyrical line he gave expression to the natural tendency of even the smallest phrase segment. Thus the motif of a rising third (in Bars 1 and 2) was played with graceful dance-like quality, subsiding in diminuendo; Bars 3 and 4 were bound together in unbroken song. Performed in this way, the theme expressed its innate warmth and animation. A Sleeping Beauty had been awakened.

Ex. 58

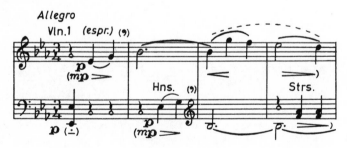

No less memorable was Casals' performance of the first orchestral statement from Beethoven's Fourth Piano Concerto:

Ex. 59

This passage came as a reverential response to the opening piano solo (movingly played by Rudolf Serkin). The first note diminished to pianissimo: 'The diminuendo brings warmth,' Casals said; the repeated quavers conveyed the most discreet forward impetus. Bars 3 and 4 were shaped individually, each arising like a sigh, each falling away. The sforzando in Bar 5 caught us unawares — a spontaneous expression of deep feeling; the descending line over Bars 5 and 6 sang unhurriedly as it yielded in intensity. The final two bars rose and fell in a gentle curve, the quaver A being touched upon tenderly. Each component of the theme had been granted its own expressive life, the arrestingly individual contours coming together to form a whole of great beauty.

Let us now take note of some instances where Casals was careful *not* to separate musical elements which belong together. Casals explained that where an appoggiatura is built into the melodic line, the note of resolution must maintain its natural connection to the appoggiatura even if not joined to it in a legato slur. The relatedness of the two notes is most often overlooked when the appoggiatura takes the form of a suspension and the note of resolution leads on to a new phrase segment. If the suspension falls off in too drastic a diminuendo the sense of continuity may easily be broken. In Exs. 60–66 Casals asked that enough tone be sustained on the suspension to ensure the unity of the phrase; the change of bow was to be negotiated without an inadvertent accent.

Ex. 60   Bach: *Brandenburg Concerto No. 6*, 2nd mvt.

Ex. 61   Bach: *Orchestral Suite No. 2*, Sarabande

Ex. 62   Beethoven: 'Eroica' *Symphony*, 1st mvt.

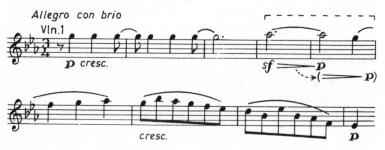

Ex. 63   Beethoven: *Symphony No. 8*, 1st mvt.

Continuity – despite the rest!

Ex. 64   Schumann: *Cello Concerto*, 1st mvt.

Ex. 65   Dvořák: *Cello Concerto*, 1st mvt.

Ex. 66   Mozart: *Symphony No. 40*, 2nd mvt.

As often played:

As interpreted by Casals:

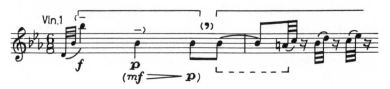

Casals was ever distinguishing between musical elements which should be separated from one another and those which should be drawn together. On occasion more than one solution is possible.

One morning he rehearsed the third movement of Mendelssohn's 'Italian' Symphony; my markings designate the external features of Casals' phrasing, but they cannot convey the spirit which guided the flow of notes, the spirit summarized in Casals' words: 'With Love!'[1]

Ex. 67a

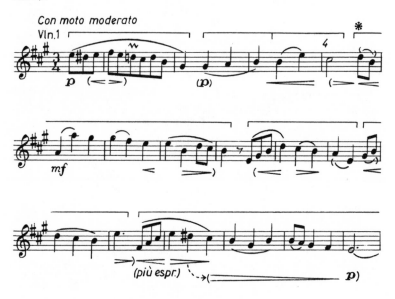

It will be noted that the quavers in Bar 4 (*) were played in crescendo; they signified the beginning of a new phrase. At the next day's rehearsal Casals said, 'Let us try another way...

[1] In an interview, Casals recalled that the music of Mendelssohn was the first love of his childhood.

perhaps it will be more beautiful.' He now requested that these
quavers be played in diminuendo: they were to conclude the
previous phrase. The new phrase was to begin with the high A in
the subsequent bar:

Ex. 67b

The two versions were equally valid, one as lovely as the other.
In literature, too, such choices are sometimes possible. Take the
speech of Hamlet, beginning 'What a piece of work is man,'
which scholars credit to Shakespeare in either of the following
constructions:

> . . . How infinite in faculty! In form and moving how express and
> admirable! In action how like an angel! In apprehension how like a
> god!

> . . . how infinite in faculties, in form and moving, how express and
> admirable in action, how like an angel in apprehension, how like a
> god.

'Finding the design' was not relegated exclusively to the shaping
of principal themes; it embraced every aspect of a composition.

Tutti passages – often treated as no more than structural 'filling
in' – were, for Casals, *living* structure. In the first movement of
Mozart's Symphony No. 40, the reiterated scales of quavers took
on shape and direction, coming each time 'with an increase in
sonority':

Ex. 68

At the climax of the development from the first movement of Mozart's Symphony No. 39, the arpeggios, played in crescendo, became urgently dramatic, leaping up like flames!

Ex. 69

'It is not enough just to play fortissimo,' Casals called out when rehearsing the following passage from Beethoven's Eighth Symphony. The strings were to accent the upper note of each successive group, the woodwind and brass to make a crescendo:

'Give life to the sustained note!' The music surged forward with irresistible power.

Ex. 70

Any student beginning to perform a series of rapid notes in a regimented, mechanical manner – no matter with what brilliance – would find himself cut short with the cry, 'No "passage work"!' Casals would then play the same notes which had just sounded so arid and methodical, revealing their expressive form. 'We must always give the design,' he would say, as when teaching Beethoven's A major Sonata:

Ex. 71

Observe in Ex. 72 the clarifications of phrasing, the variations of texture. My notation cannot capture the charm of the subtle rubato.

Ex. 72   Haydn: *Cello Concerto in D major*, 1st mvt.

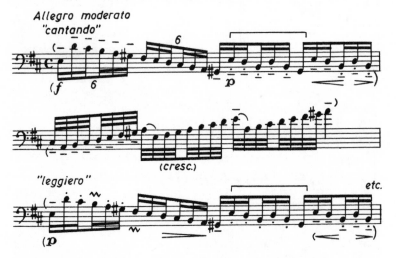

The word *cantando* was ever at his lips. The violins' descending scale figure in Mozart's Symphony No. 39 was to be 'singing on every note'.

Ex. 73

How often would he exclaim: 'It's not a "passage" – it's a *wonderful melody*!'

Ex. 74   Beethoven: *Cello Sonata in C Major*, Finale

Allegro vivace

Above all, Casals hated that which was sterile, cold and life-less. A 'correct' performance held no interest for him if it failed to communicate the essential glory of music, its ability, through the beauty of its contours, the depth and range of its expression, to move us to the heart. When confronted with a student unwilling to make an interpretative commitment, Casals would say: 'It is even better to do something in bad taste than to be monotonous.'

Two months before his death, Casals, then in his ninety-seventh year, conducted a youth orchestra in Israel. 'I am a very, very, very old musician,' he told the young instrumentalists. 'I am the oldest musician today.' He proceeded to rehearse Mozart's Symphony No. 33 with ageless vitality, communicating the irrepressible elemental force of his ecstatic love for music. '*Con amore – con amore*,' he urged, going over a particular phrase a dozen times; 'otherwise it means nothing – it's against the music!' 'Repetition in music means more piano or more forte – like when you are speaking; in music it's the same – give expression, and then *more* expression!' 'The highest note must be heard – like *singing* – mezzo forte at least. It is not marked in the score; that doesn't matter. There are one thousand things that are not marked!' he thundered. 'Don't give notes – give the meaning of the notes!'

CHAPTER III

DICTION FOR INSTRUMENTALISTS

Diminuendo is the life of music.

A horse! a horse! my kingdom for a horse!

T HE quotation is famous enough, but how should one deliver the line most effectively?

One need not be in the predicament of Richard III to realize that what matters most is not how loudly nine simple words can be shouted, but the sharpness of impact of the more important words as they fall upon the ear. Let me restate this self-evident principle, making use of markings of musical expression. Let us suppose the words to be spoken at a sustained level of volume:

A HORSE A HORSE MY KINGDOM FOR A HORSE

*sempre ff*_____

Or, by contrast, with an articulation corresponding to the natural inflections of speech:

A Horse! a Horse! my Kingdom for a Horse!

$<sf> <sf> < sf > < sf>$

If the reader experiments by saying the line aloud, he may wish to vary the degree of stress placed upon each sforzando, perhaps by granting special importance to 'kingdom' or by emphasizing the equestrian invocations. Whichever way he chooses, he will instinctively render each sforzando intelligible by a subsequent decrease in volume – or, in terms of music, a diminuendo.

Casals often commented on the relationship between music and the spoken word. 'An accented note,' he said, 'will stand out and keep its value, not so much because of its special intensity but principally because of the shade which succeeds it. These remarks find a parallel in a law of nature: let us shout very loud and observe the endless diminuendo which follows. The performance of music cannot exclude this most natural reality.' By way of illustration he would call out 'Hey!' and go on to explain that 'when we make this effort in giving an accent, our lungs are emptied quickly. We give *all* – and a diminuendo comes. This is exactly the same with the notes.'

'Lightning!' Casals exclaimed, describing the entrance of the cello in the Saint-Saëns A minor Concerto. He pointed out that after the initial attack the intensity of the first note should be diminished. 'If you continue the forte you don't hear the accent. A strong accent must have a diminuendo: then it is more powerful and more natural.' He demonstrated as follows:

Ex. 75

This diminuendo has significance not only for the first note but for the second note as well, in that it permits the D to be better heard. Thus, where clear articulation is required, the diminuendo fulfils a dual function: it gives definition to the note on which it occurs and enables us to bring the following note into relief.

Let us now apply our Richard III elocution test to the delineation of phrasing in the development section from the first movement of Beethoven's Eighth Symphony. The following passage is marked *ff* with an *sf* at the beginning of the second phrase. First we shall sustain the tone throughout:

Ex. 76a

And now, in keeping with Casals' interpretation, we will begin fortissimo, allow the first phrase to end in a diminuendo, then attack the following sforzando with renewed energy:

Ex. 76b

Ex. 76b reveals a notable gain in clarity. Casals would explain: 'A diminuendo gives interest to what follows; an accent has more importance by contrast. The inflection on one note gives value to the next.'

The relevance of this principle is further exemplified on the subsequent page of the score where this phrase comes in for contrapuntal treatment. Casals obtained from the orchestra a breathtaking incisiveness of accentuation and transparency of texture. It is evident that 'Richard's himself again'.

Ex. 76c

Many performers today feel that to 'give way' in the manner Casals suggested will have a weakening effect, and that (particularly in Beethoven) a continuously sustained *ff* will give a better impression of strength. In fact, although the diminuendi indicated suggest a decrease in *volume* there was no decrease in *intensity*; the music has never been set forth with more rugged grandeur.

The following passages, in forte and piano respectively, call for distinct enunciation. A diminuendo on the first note enhances the vitality of both the first and second notes:

Ex. 77 Haydn: *Symphony No. 95, 1st mvt.*

Ex. 78 Mozart: *Symphony No. 35, 1st mvt.*

In the principal theme of the Finale of the Dvořák Cello Concerto, a 'natural diminuendo' imbues each crotchet with decisiveness and penetrating power.

Ex. 79

When playing the following passage from the opening movement of this work, Casals rendered the accentuation of the E (first note in Bar 3) more effective by means of a decrescendo over the preceding semiquavers. 'In this way we have more colour – contrast.'

Ex. 80

For Casals, the value inherent in what he referred to as 'the law of the diminuendo' was essential to the communication of music — as it is to speech. Nevertheless, he found that many musicians seriously underestimate its importance. We tend to be inhibited by the printed score with its scarcity of expressive markings; the beauty of our tone production may lead us to forget that uniformity breeds monotony. We too often confuse sustained power with expressive elucidation. Furthermore, when we think we are playing with sufficient dynamic contrast, we may, in fact, not be doing so, as we soon discover when we hear recordings of our performance. An invaluable lesson of Casals' teaching was to alert the ear and the bow arm to the fact that clear articulation in music demands a far greater range of dynamic inflection than we normally realize. Casals would remind his students: 'In playing a passage in forte with natural accents, you arrive to piano — so that this forte has variety. This is a simple rule but it is not generally known.' Bearing this in mind, we can better understand that certain diminuendi which might seem exaggerated to the instrumentalist may not necessarily sound exaggerated to the listener.[1]

Casals had an uncanny ability to listen to the actual sound he was producing. Intention to be clear was not enough. Absolute clarity of articulation was a canon of his artistry. He often gave credit to an essential factor in achieving this goal: 'Diminuendo is the life of music.'

[1] In *Science and Music* Sir James Jeans describes experiments which reveal that 'generally speaking . . . our ears are insensitive to anything less than a 25 per cent difference of energy. The pianist who is executing a rapid passage may allow himself a 25 per cent variation in the strengths of different notes, without our ears detecting any falling off from regularity. The organ-voicer may leave a row of pipes differing by as much as 25 per cent in strength, and even a trained ear will pass them as perfectly uniform.'

Let us now turn to further tasks performed by the diminuendo in the service of musical diction, most significantly in the elucidation of repeated notes and ornaments.[1]

'When a note is repeated,' Casals counselled, 'it is important that the beginning of the second note should be clearly heard. A natural diminuendo at the end of the first note gives *value* to the second note.' Thus, in the following examples, the decrescendo allows the second note to be enunciated distinctly without recourse to exaggerated accentuation; clarification is achieved while retaining grace.

Ex. 81.   Haydn: *Cello Concerto in D major*, 1st mvt.

Ex. 82.   Dvořák: *Cello Concerto*, Finale

In Ex. 83 we see how Casals applied this principle even when a series of repeated notes is formed into a crescendo. He ensured note-to-note clarity by giving the semiquavers individual

---

[1] These problems are particularly acute for the string and wind player, less so for the pianist. The pianist's difficulties increase when he wishes to have his percussion instrument imitate the legato which his string- and wind-playing colleagues can produce with ease.

diminuendi. Each successive note began with increased strength, the last semiquaver carrying the crescendo over to the bar line.

Ex. 83 Beethoven: *Cello Sonata in A major*, 3rd mvt.

In certain cases, particularly when a dotted rhythm was present, Casals would bring to repeated notes a release and renewal of intensity, the second note coming as an upbeat to the music that followed:

Ex. 84 Beethoven: *Cello Sonata in A major*, 3rd mvt.

Ex. 85 Beethoven: *Symphony No. 4*, 4th mvt.

Ex. 86 Dvořák: *Cello Concerto*, 1st mvt.

A similar approach was brought to bear on the repeated notes which occur in the sorrow-laden theme which opens Schumann's Fourth Symphony; each successive phrase begins on the same note with which the previous phrase has ended.

Ex. 87

Conducting in expressive quaver beats which drew from the orchestra the most beautiful legato playing, Casals' gesture changed radically at the instant of the juncture between phrases. In a sudden, tiny movement his hands lurched forward. Without break in continuity, the new phrase was born of a throbbing impulse, betraying the agitation which underlies the whole passage.

Just before the première of 'The Ring', Richard Wagner issued a 'last request' in a handwritten note to the singers:

!*Clarity*!
The big notes come of themselves; it is
the little notes that require attention . . .

A prime function of the diminuendo is indeed to bring the attention of the ear to the little notes. When one or more short notes follow a longer note, an intervening diminuendo provides the bridge to clarification, as in the following passage from the Finale of the Schumann Cello Concerto:

Ex. 88

Where the little notes are included within the same legato slur (i.e. without a change of bow), as in Ex. 89:

Ex. 89   Beethoven: *Cello Sonata in C major*, 1st mvt.

considerable demands are made upon the flexibility and responsiveness of the bow arm. With the diminuendo comes a slowing of bow speed and release of pressure; the subsequent accentuation on the first of the little notes requires a quickening of bow speed and re-exertion of pressure. Casals emphasized that this process should be carried out *without stopping the bow* at the end of the diminuendo. In this way the continuity of line remains unbroken; the articulation has a natural resilience, never sounding ungainly or crude.

While the precise degree of accentuation will vary according to the context in which it appears, the principle of achieving clarity by means of the diminuendo retains its validity, whether in a passage of exquisite lyricism:

Ex. 90   Schubert: *Symphony No. 4*, 2nd mvt.

or of 'passionate declamation':

Ex. 91   Mendelssohn: *'Italian' Symphony*, 2nd mvt.

The result obtained in music is akin to the effect produced by
chiaroscuro in painting. By delicate juxtaposition of light and
shade the artist may create the impression of perspective on canvas; the figures will seem to be modelled in a third dimension. By
moulding his intensities by means of dynamic contrast the instrumentalist will bring points of emphasis into the foreground,
giving a sense of depth and relief to the musical line.

Where the short notes are not preceded by a long note – there
being little or no possibility of making a diminuendo in prepara-
tion for the accent – the difficulty in achieving good articulation
is increased. At such times Casals, whether in a cello lesson or
orchestral rehearsal, was relentless and unremitting in his quest
for every note to be heard distinctly. Ornaments can be problematical in this respect. 'Remember,' he would say, 'that the first
note of an ornament must receive an accent; otherwise it is lost!'

In the second movement of the Boccherini Cello Sonata in A
major, the ornaments were to be 'more accented than the real
notes'.

Ex. 92a

Ex. 92b

Ex. 92c

It was rare for a student to clear the hurdle of the second subject of the opening movement of Brahms' E minor Sonata without being stopped (if not also for a host of other reasons) because he had failed to pronounce the first note of the turn with sufficient vitality.

Ex. 93

And it seemed as if the Marlboro Festival Orchestra – the most alert and vigorous of ensembles – would never get beyond the opening bar when rehearsing the third movement of Mendelssohn's 'Italian' Symphony, so insistent was Casals that the ornament be rendered with maximum clarity. 'Be daring with your bows!' the eighty-six-year-old man challenged his younger colleagues.

Ex. 94

But we should not leave our discussion of the diminuendo as an agent of clarification without mentioning some of its other roles in this respect; for instance, its usefulness in lightening the texture of long notes in an accompaniment figure:

Ex. 95   Beethoven: *'Archduke' Trio, Op. 97,* 3rd mvt.

Ex. 96   Mendelssohn: *'Italian' Symphony,* 3rd mvt.

its service in articulating syncopations:

Ex. 97   Mozart: *Symphony No. 38,* 1st mvt.

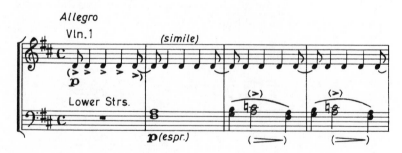

Ex. 98   Wagner: '*Siegfried Idyll*'

or, as already touched upon in Chapter II, its function in bringing economy to a crescendo:

Ex. 99   Mozart: *Symphony No. 40*, Finale

Casals reminisced: 'I have heard so many violinists and cellists –
and they are *wonderful*. And afterwards you say, "How curious;
he plays so well, but, I don't know . . . I feel monotony, lack of
variety; he doesn't colour enough".' In his teaching Casals would
frequently exclaim: 'Look at the colour on this note: let us give
the natural accent!' or, 'Without a diminuendo it's flat; it has no
interest. It's a wonderful thing – every note must have life!' Even
when legato is the predominant interpretative element, Casals
would often say: 'The little notes must *speak*'; they were to be
given clear enunciation within the lyrical line, as in the opening
theme of Brahms' E minor Sonata (see Ex. 26).

For Casals, the accentuation of an ornament held a
significance even beyond the imperative act of clarification. He

asked a student to imagine the following phrase *without* the grace
note which the composer has placed before the E in the final bar:

Ex. 100   Dvořák: *Cello Concerto,* 1st mvt.

He then played the phrase – expansively, ardently – bringing it
to its point of expressive culmination *with* the addition of the
grace note. 'You see how beautiful it is! The ornament is the *exaltation of the note*! This is why it must have an accent. Don't be
afraid to play it frankly!'

Having observed the manner in which Casals brought clarity
to individual notes, let us turn to another problem in musical diction, that of bringing clarity to the concluding notes of a phrase
which ends in a diminuendo. Here the requirement is not to
differentiate one note from another by means of a rapid
diminuendo, but, rather, to ensure the continuity of the melodic
line by not becoming too soft too soon. 'Every note must be
clear!' was an irrevocable command. Even the softest note of a
phrase was to retain vitality.

When, in Mozart's Symphony No. 40, Casals asked that expressive emphasis be placed upon the first note of the motif:

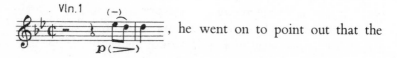, he went on to point out that the

second note (the quaver D), although softer than the first,
'must also be heard'. The phrase was rehearsed until just the
right dynamic relationship was attained.

In the Larghetto from Beethoven's Second Symphony he directed the violins not to become so soft on the B♯ as to exclude the possibility for yet further diminuendo on the C♯.

Ex. 101

While Casals considered it natural that a descending line should be characterized by a decrescendo, he none the less asked the violins to keep tone when playing the following scale passage from Schubert's Fifth Symphony, thus ensuring that the notes which enter into the low tessitura were not lost to the ear.

Ex. 102

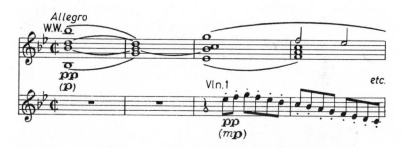

A piano following immediately on the heels of a forte will often sound too soft because of the sudden contrast in dynamics. In such cases Casals took special care to make the necessary compensation by increasing the dynamic level of the piano. In Exs. 103 and 104 the violins were asked to translate their *fp* accordingly, sustaining tone at first and only gradually decreasing in intensity:

Ex. 103   Beethoven: *Symphony No. 4*, 2nd mvt.

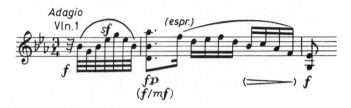

Ex. 104   Mendelssohn: *'Italian' Symphony*, 1st mvt.

In the first movement of Schubert's 'Unfinished' Symphony the violas, although marked *p*, were to enter after the *ff* tutti in *mf*. In the theme which follows, Casals asked the violins to transfer the diminuendo to the subsequent bar; the melody was to be granted its full expansion. The crotchet D was 'still to be heard even though it comes in diminuendo'.

Ex. 105

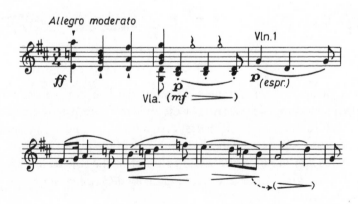

Casals often drew attention to the relativity of the term 'piano'. When a student would begin the Schumann Concerto or the Brahms E minor Sonata too softly, Casals would say, 'Piano, yes — but don't be timid. We must know that it is the beginning of a melody!'

This brings us to a question of musical interpretation to which Casals accorded the greatest significance; namely, the enunciation of the first note.

When we study the illuminated manuscripts of the Middle Ages, we are constantly amazed at the artistic beauty of the first letter of each paragraph. The great majority of these texts are of a religious nature; on each page is inscribed a sacred revelation. The elaboration of the initial was understood to be the visible manifestation of the divine impulse. For this reason illuminators were engaged to embellish these letters in red, gold, or sometimes blue.

For Casals, the first note was the portal through which the divine impulse entered our earthly domain. His means of imparting this immediate sense of presence were subtle and variable.[1] Fortunately, many vivid reminders of this characteristic aspect of Casals' artistry are preserved on recordings. We find such an example in his supremely beautiful and simple statement of the theme of the Andante from Schubert's Bb major Trio (in the recording with Thibaud and Cortot). When listening to the very first sound emanating from Casals' cello, we know what it is when matter is born of spirit.

Ex. 106

[1] See Chapter V.

[2] Note on the recording the artistry with which Casals varies the inflections within this theme, obviating any sense of identical accentuation.

In all Casals' teaching or playing, no first initial of a musical paragraph remained untouched by the illuminator's art. 'The first note is not gay enough!' he would often call out at the beginning of a Bach dance movement in major key. Or, 'We must feel in the first note the tragic character of the piece!' when commencing the Prelude to the C minor Suite. When rehearsing a pianissimo passage from the opening movement of the 'Italian' Symphony: 'Even here the first note has to be heard – sing at once!' A transitional string figure, which usually receives no special attention, glistened as if limned in gold.

From time to time on some of Casals' late recordings we hear a groan of emotion breaking forth from him just before he begins to play a phrase. This is the audible, human expression of the spirit which moves him, which *precedes* the music and from which emerges the musical communication. The moral for string players is not that they should moan audibly – at least not before they are eighty – but that it is the will of the gods that they should never touch bow to string with indifference.

CHAPTER IV

PERCEIVING TIME RELATIONSHIPS

Fantasy as much as you like – but with order!

THE orchestra was poised to begin rehearsing the slow movement of Beethoven's Fourth Symphony when Casals turned
to the second violins who were about to play the figure:

Ex. 107a

and said, 'The art of interpretation is *not* to play what is written.'
In these words Casals was stating a fundamental tenet of his
music-making.

Since earliest times, song and dance have arisen freely and spontaneously, conveying messages of the human spirit which cannot
otherwise be expressed. When, over the course of history, it was
deemed useful to find ways of notating melody and rhythm, such
markings were never meant to be representative of music itself in
all its natural life, vigour and subtlety. Indeed, there is an old
adage, not without truth: 'When music is written down, it dies.'
The printed score is like a landscape painted on a cardboard
façade; houses, trees and hills stand stiffly side by side. These
lifeless images are no more than symbols of a deeper artistic
reality; they invite the interpreter to discover the world of
experience of which they are the mere semblance. When the

re-creative spirit of the performer leads us through one of the painted doors, we suddenly find ourselves entering a three-dimensional realm. The forms take on depth. We perceive the movement of light and shadow. The air may be fresh with spring moisture or still, as in the last days of autumn. Here, beyond the façade, the houses caress the hillside like certain Andalusian villages which flow so naturally into the contour of their surroundings as to resemble the shapes of streams. In these villages the dwellings are related to one another by cohesive design born of instinctive feeling.

'The written note,' Casals has said, 'is like a strait jacket, whereas music, like life itself, is constant movement, continuous spontaneity, free from any restriction . . . There are so many excellent instrumentalists who are completely obsessed by the printed note, whereas it has a very limited power to express what the music actually means.'

Casals states here no more than what many other musicians have observed in the past. François Couperin noted, in 1717, 'We write otherwise than we perform'; Liszt commented, 'Notation, in spite of painstaking conscientiousness, can never fully suffice . . . certain features – among them the most important ones – cannot be put down in writing.'

The vitality of a musical performance is dependent upon the spontaneous feeling for rhythm communicated by the interpreter. Yet rhythm is not only difficult to fix in notation; it even resists satisfactory definition. 'What is rhythm?' asked Vaughan Williams; and he proceeded to quote Lord Haldane's epigram: 'I cannot define an elephant, but I recognize one when I see it.' 'In the same way,' V.W. continued, 'without being able to explain it, those who are naturally musical can appreciate rhythm, or the want of it, in a piece of music.'

But let us return to the Adagio from Beethoven's Fourth Symphony. Casals sang the rhythmic figure to be played by the second violins, instinctively moving each demisemiquaver slightly closer to the subsequent semiquaver; the rests being, in consequence, imperceptibly elongated. There was to be no question of exaggeration; no more than a minute alteration was called for. Yet, when the passage was played in this way, the relationship of short note to long note became subtly more buoyant and alive. It should be emphasized that these rhythmic fluctuations took place within the framework of the main beat; the basic pulse remained constant. In between the regularly occurring quaver beats, the waves of movement were allowed to follow their inherent pattern of ebb and flow.[1]

Ex. 107b

Throughout history, musicians have observed that dotted rhythms, in particular, are poorly served by notation. Leopold Mozart tells us of certain passages 'where the dot is to be held rather longer . . . if the performance is not to sound too sleepy'. And, two centuries later, Bruno Walter comments, 'The measurability of musical rhythm, and therefore the accurateness of its notation, is only approximate . . .. Divergence from arithmetical exactness occurs mainly in the case of the short notes in dotted rhythms, which an interpreter of lively rhythmic sense feels a little shorter, and therefore places a little later than prescribed by notation.'

In passages such as the following, the 'natural rhythm' that Casals requested had a radically energizing effect in contrast to the written note-values which he sometimes described as 'no rhythm at all':

[1] The arrows which I have placed above the musical examples are meant to suggest the extent and directional tendency of these subtle currents of movement.

Ex. 108   Beethoven: *Piano Concerto No. 4*, 2nd mvt.

Ex. 109   Brahms: *Cello Sonata in F major*, 1st mvt.

Ex. 110   Dvořák: *Cello Concerto*, 2nd mvt.

The pattern ♪♪ ♩ or ♫♪ is another figure which, Casals believed, often needs to be freed from bondage to the printed page. The two shorter notes, he observed, usually belong together in a slightly quicker grouping than the score indicates. Beethoven's pupil Czerny tells us that the composer played this rhythmic pattern, where it occurs in the Finale of his First Piano Concerto, in such a manner that the two semiquavers were condensed into a more rapid unit of time, 'more as:

than [as notated]:  '

The precise extent to which the short notes are compressed will vary with the spirit of a work.[1] Tightly knit semiquavers give a dash of gypsy flavour to the first of Schumann's 'Fünf Stücke im Volkston', Op. 102:

Ex. 111

and enliven Mephisto's gait in Couperin's 'Air de Diable':

Ex. 112

A subtler application of the principle will impart just the needed rhythmic vitality to the Scherzo from Beethoven's 'Archduke' Trio, Op. 97:

Ex. 113

[1] In Exs. 111–114 the very small amount of time gained by quickening the semiquavers (or quavers as the case may be) is compensated for by a minute break between the note groupings, as indicated by the symbol (/).

and affirm the out-of-doors exuberance at the beginning of the
Finale of the Elgar Cello Concerto:

Ex. 114

Mozart's demisemiquavers in the Andante from his Symphony
No. 40:

Ex. 115

are that shade more exquisite when played 'just a little faster than
written' (the semiquaver rests being, therefore, a fraction longer
than notated).

The Trio from the third movement of Mendelssohn's 'Italian'
Symphony contains the two rhythmic patterns which we have
been considering. Casals asked that each of these be played 'in a
natural way', the barely perceptible transformation of time-
values creating what he called 'a rhythm that satisfies'.

Ex. 116

Where a group of short notes is preceded by a long dotted note, the principles of clear articulation and enlivened rhythm both come into play. Casals would ask that the dotted note have a diminuendo and be prolonged; the short notes were to be delicately accented and a little quickened in time. In this way the principal theme from the slow movement of Mozart's G major Flute Concerto assumed its inherent grace:

Ex. 117

while Bach's lament 'Ach, nun ist mein Jesus hin' (Ah, now is my Jesus gone) from the St. Matthew Passion pierced to the very heart:

Ex. 118

In the hushed, sorrowful atmosphere of the second movement
of Beethoven's Cello Sonata in D major:

Ex. 119

the intuitive placement of the demisemiquavers a fraction late
gives just the right feeling of expressive tension. 'Those things
cannot be printed,' Casals would say, 'but the meaning is this;
this has character.'

Casals did not always quicken the short notes when playing
dotted rhythms. He would point out that every rhythmic pattern
has to be considered in reference to its specific setting. In another
passage from the slow movement of Beethoven's D major
Sonata, he said: 'In this case we must give the real value of the
notes. Here it is a song; every note sings.'

Ex. 120

In Ex. 121 Casals considered that every note has melodic significance; he would linger expressively upon the first demisemiquaver.

Ex. 121   Beethoven: *Cello Sonata in A major*, 3rd mvt.

Casals often drew attention to extended series of notes which belong together in a single wave of movement. Certain musical phrases possess an élan which can only be released through an act of rhythmic concision. For Casals, the first movement of Beethoven's Eighth Symphony was an expression of Dionysian joy. He took this movement at a rollicking pace, conceiving the pulsation basically in one beat per bar rather than in the traditional three.[1] Right at the outset he insisted upon internal cohesion for each of the two rhythmic groupings which subsequently appear throughout the movement:

Ex. 122a

and Ex. 122b

He persistently rehearsed the rising scale (Ex. 122b) until the quavers conveyed 'no semblance of separate notes'.[2] The result was a performance of stunning exhilaration, as if a broom had swept away the cobwebs of tired tradition, revealing the passage in the freshness of its first creation. Similarly, in the reoccurring figure:

Ex. 123

[1] Observe the composer's exceptional tempo marking: *Allegro vivace e con brio*.
[2] In saying this, Casals was referring to perception of rhythm, not articulation. The individual quavers were short and clearly articulated; they were to be felt as one uninterrupted rhythmic unit.

he conceived the four notes as belonging together. The rhythmic change could hardly be measured by a metronome, yet what an enormous sense of presence it instilled in the playing!

One is reminded of Artur Schnabel who, characteristically, grouped the chords at the beginning of Beethoven's 'Hammerklavier' Sonata in such a way that the opening bars burst forth tumultuously.

Ex. 124

In the first movement of Beethoven's D Major Cello Sonata, Casals brought to the figure:

Ex. 125

an intense concentration of energy; the semiquavers were drawn tightly together, becoming a motif in themselves. An instant's break, before the high note, allowed the bow to be lifted in order to give a forceful attack to the sforzando. This phrase sprang at one like a tiger. In the subject of the Finale of the same work:

Ex. 126

the initial crotchet stood alone, as if posing a question. The quavers were gathered into one upbeat group, alighting at the first delicate point of accentuation on the downbeat of the succeeding bar, which served as a springboard for the syncopation.[1]

When conducting the second movement of Mozart's Symphony No. 39, Casals elicited in the dramatic F minor passage a performance of fierce intensity, heightened by his insistence that each phrase be played concisely: 'as one idea — rapidly!'

Ex. 127

This was not a performance designed to enshrine the image of Mozart as the composer of perpetual serenity.

If rhythm tends to elude precise definition, *tempo rubato* is a veritable fugitive.

Casals considered rubato to be an inherent factor in music of all periods. His practice in this respect was at variance with the at-

---

[1] The presto theme from the first movement of Haydn's 'Clock' Symphony has similar attributes:

Igor Stravinsky advises the interpreter here to build a 'measure-and-a-note upbeat . . . avoiding not only a strong but also a weak downbeat on the first measure, and saving the thesis for the second full measure.'

titude prevalent during the first part of this century, exemplified by *Grove's Dictionary* which, until its third edition, published when Casals was fifty, advised that rubato 'is allowable in the works of all the modern "romantic" masters, from Weber downwards ... In the case of the older masters, it is entirely and unconditionally inadmissible.'[1] Musicology eventually caught up with Casals. The present edition of *Grove's Dictionary* describes rubato as 'the free element in time' without restricting its use to any historical period.

Casals' feeling for *tempo rubato* was determined, not by presupposed rules and regulations about musical epochs, but by the specific character of the individual work. For instance, while he generally taught that the poetic fantasy-world of Schumann seeks expression by means of an eloquent rubato, he none the less asked his students to play Exs. 128 and 129 without altering the rhythmic values; these pieces were to be set forth in all simplicity.

Ex. 128   Schumann: *'Fünf Stücke im Volkston', No. 2*

Ex. 129   Schumann: *'Fünf Stücke im Volkston', No. 3*

[1] *Grove's* notwithstanding, Couperin spoke of 'the spirit, the soul' that must be added to the mere 'quantity and time-value of the beats'; C. P. E. Bach instructed that 'certain purposeful violations of the beat are often exceptionally beautiful.'

Casals likened the slow movement of Beethoven's Cello Sonata in D major to a 'funeral march'. The following passage was to move in absolutely regular time.

Ex. 130

In contrast, he played the Boccherini B♭ major Concerto with considerable freedom. This music is exemplary of 'the purest rococo . . . more rococo than Mozart − or even Haydn'. Showing how one may linger for a moment on the upper notes of a phrase, he would exclaim: 'If we sing we do that. Let us do it with the instrument also. It is such a guide − such a wonderful guide − the voice!'

Ex. 131

The agogic accents (i.e. prolongations of length not necessarily supported by dynamic stress) noted in Ex. 131 do not arrest the overall sense of movement; they evoke a compensatory motion which restores the rhythmic balance of the phrase. As Casals has said, 'Time lost on expressive accents being placed on the first note of a group, or on the highest note, is to be regained by the intervening notes.'[1]

---

[1] Tosi expressed this principle in his classic treatise, *Observations on the Florid Song . . . Useful for all Performers, Instrumental as well as Vocal* (trans. by Galliard, 1743): 'The stealing of Time . . . is an honorable Theft in one that sings better than others, provided he makes a Restitution with Ingenuity.'

Casals' rubato was founded on an extraordinarily subtle give and take of time-values; it defies adequate description and my efforts in this regard must be viewed as no more than approximations. I am in the position of a medieval theologian seeking to specify the weight of an angel. How right was Leopold Mozart when he wrote: 'What this stolen time is can more easily be shown than described.'

Let us give consideration to the role of agogic accents in various musical contexts. With the subtle elongation of but one or two notes within a bar Casals could work wonders, giving expressive breadth to the beginning of a piece:

Ex. 132   Bach: *Solo Cello Suite No. 2*, Prelude

lending the crest of a phrase a soaring grace:

Ex. 133   Haydn: *Cello Concerto in D major*, 1st mvt.

differentiating notes of special melodic or harmonic significance:

Ex. 134   Schumann: *Cello Concerto*, 1st mvt.

bringing diversity to a melody built in sequential phrases:

Ex. 135   Schumann: *'Adagio and Allegro', Op. 70*

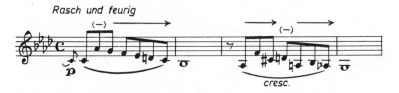

revealing the lyric soul concealed within a melody consisting of note-values of similar printed length:

Ex. 136   Brahms: *Cello Sonata in F major,* 3rd mvt.

enhancing the singing quality of a short note which has been dwarfed by a preceding long note:

Ex. 137   Beethoven: *Cello Sonata in F major,* 1st mvt.

In Ex. 137 the agogic accent serves several additional purposes. It designates the importance of the second minim beat within the bar, expresses the appoggiatura (B♭ —A), avoids monotony in the quavers, and confers roundness upon the descending scale.

   In the above examples the reciprocity of time-values is completed within the span of each bar. We must also speak of *tempo rubato* extending over an entire phrase – of the manner in which Casals delineated the dual character of the following passage from the Finale of Beethoven's C major Sonata:

Ex. 138

the triplet quavers stealing time as they cast up a rainbow bridge; the semiquavers then entering full of high spirits, as though in playful surprise. Or of the Homeric grandeur with which he played the cello entrance in Beethoven's D major Sonata:

Ex. 139

In the opening arpeggio we heard no ordinary quavers, but the steps of Hector mounting to the parapet; the ensuing melody was no mere three bars, but a vision of an heroic landscape, compressed within time; the sonority was open and noble, the quaver G being proclaimed spaciously – 'frankly'.

Casals rarely 'explained' rubato; he would customarily play or sing the phrase in question. Thus it was of considerable interest to hear him offer specific advice on the subject when, in the Finale of Schumann's Fourth Symphony, he directed the woodwind to 'anticipate' the first of their triplet quavers by entering a hair's breadth earlier than marked in the score.

Ex. 140

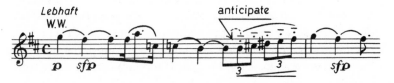

This gave room for the ascending scale to be declaimed freely, without disturbing the fundamental tempo.[1]

For Casals, any definition of *tempo rubato* had to include awareness of proportion. He followed in the tradition of such masters as Mozart and Chopin, both of whom are known to have allowed the melodic line freedom of expression while respecting the underlying rhythmic continuity.[2]

Those who have been privileged to see Margot Fonteyn dance will have witnessed such rubato in visual form. At the apogee of lyric intensity she would seem, during an infinitesimal moment, suspended in space, before flowing again into the rhythmic unity of the whole. In the same way Casals would lift a phrase to a moment of timeless beauty, while continuing to make us aware of the rhythmic values of the entire movement.

'Do you see those trees?' Liszt once asked a pupil. 'The wind toys with their leaves, it develops life among them; the trees remain the same; that is Chopin's rubato.' It was Casals' rubato as well.

Finding that young musicians, in general, either lack courage to play freely, or else tend to transform liberty into licence, Casals offered his students a golden rule of interpretation: 'Fantasy as much as you like – but with order!' Typically, he would

[1] See also Beethoven's Pastoral Symphony, Chapter VII, p. 186.

[2] C. P. E. Bach, too, understood such matters: 'When the execution is such that one hand seems to play against the bar and the other strictly with it, it may be said that the performer is doing everything that can be required of him.'

make a comparison with life. 'We talk of democracy and freedom – but with order. You cannot just do anything you wish; music is the same.'

This rule applied to every departure from rhythmic regularity. For instance, when executing ritardandi, the performer must take care to avoid weakening the architectural spans with which the rhythmic structure of a work is built. The transitional bars from the first movement of the Dvořák Cello Concerto usually suffer in just this way.

Ex. 141

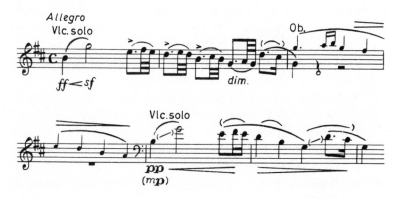

'The whole passage is too long if we make a ritardando,' Casals counselled, 'a diminuendo is enough' – a statement often heard from Casals in varying musical contexts.

In those passages in the second movement of the same work where the composer has indicated a ritardando, as in the following example:

Ex. 142

Casals cautioned against allowing the tempo to become too slow too soon; the ritardando was to proceed 'in a very regular way – with order and balance. . . . Otherwise we are lost – and the public also!'

In music of an improvisatory nature – fantasies, recitatives, cadenzas and the like – the very diversity of musical ideas obliges the performer to establish convincing proportions. 'Although it is a cadenza,' Casals would say, 'one must feel a certain logic . . . not a disordered fantasy.'

The principle of *fantasy with order* also expressed itself in terms of rhythmic stress. In the first bars of the Saint-Saëns Cello Concerto in A minor, Casals extended the slur across the bar line the better to express the natural urge of the phrase. As, furthermore, the decisive stresses within the melody fall upon syncopations, Casals pointed out that the listener requires a reminder of the metric pulsation. He therefore gave clear enunciation to the C which begins the second bar: 'Just a little accent in the middle so as to have equilibrium in the whole thing.'

Ex. 143

Similarly, in the following passage from the first movement of the Dvořák Cello Concerto he advised placing an accent on every half bar. 'You must not lose the rhythm; you must know where you are':

Ex. 144

In Ex. 145 he called for a robust accentuation on the first note of each bar in order to preserve the sense of 3/4 time and, in so doing, bring variety to the repetition of rhythmic values.

Ex. 145   Beethoven: *Symphony No. 8*, 1st mvt.

Casals described the interpretative challenge of rhythmic organization in all of its diverse aspects as 'the sense of measuring time in space'. By this he meant the ability of the performer to apprehend the relatedness between the small units of time, such as we have been discussing, and the larger time spans – the group-ings of phrases and major structural features – of which a work is composed. The performer must possess an overall vision com-parable to that of the medieval builders of Chartres Cathedral who invested every panel of stained glass with individual character, while not forgetting that a whole window tells a parable, that all the windows are related architecturally and spiritually to one another and, indeed, to the sculpture on the exterior. The great composers, like these craftsmen, wished us to experience concurrently the validity of the parts and of the whole. The musician must ascertain the most comprehensive vantage point which allows the simultaneous perception of the value inherent in each dimension. This vantage point is his choice of tempo.

Casals' tempi often came as revelations to the present generation. This resulted not only from his performing a given work faster or slower than we are accustomed to hearing it, but from the life-energy which each tempo conveyed, rooted as it was in Casals' way of understanding the unit of pulse which best expresses the music's content. The music of Brahms provides a notable case in point. 'Brahms' tempi are very often misunderstood,' Casals explained. Taking as an example the Finale of the Double Concerto:

Ex. 146

he pointed out that Brahms himself conceived this work not in pulsations of crotchets but of quavers, with a consequent moderating effect upon the actual speed. 'For us, ordinarily, it would be andante; for Brahms it is *Vivace non troppo*. Why? Because he counts the eighths. This is very necessary to know; this is why Brahms is very often – nearly always – played too fast.'

When a student began the Scherzo from Brahms' F major Sonata at a precipitous pace, Casals demonstrated how the vitality of rhythm is actually enhanced when the quaver is felt as the underlying unit of pulse. 'This is what counts: every note – every eighth!'

Ex. 147

The ear, now alerted to the motion of individual quavers, has the impression of quickness of movement, despite the decrease in velocity. 'This has a different character; this is the Brahms tempo.' There was now no need to play the expressive melody of the middle section more slowly; it followed 'naturally, in the same tempo'.

Ex. 148

The 6/8 Vivace from Brahms' 'St. Antoni' Variations:

Ex. 149

is taken by most present-day conductors at an extremely rapid pace. 'Brahms, as well as Schumann, thought of these time signatures as meaning quite different things,' Casals explained. 'We must play in six-eight, not two-four.' In other words, we should feel the weight of the quavers which come between the dotted crotchet beats.[1]

---

[1] When Casals conducted this work in London in 1927, his tempo for this variation engendered critical controversy, A. H. Fox Strangways, music critic of *The Observer* and founder of *Music and Letters,* had the last word. Having known Brahms, he attested to the validity of Casals' tempo.

'You know how I dislike quarrelling about tempo,' wrote Schumann, 'and how for me the inner measure of the movement is the sole distinguishing factor. Thus the faster adagio of a cold performer always sounds lazier than the slowest adagio of a warm-blooded interpreter.'

When teaching the last movement of the Schumann Cello Concerto (see Ex. 88), Casals insisted upon a tempo (in this case marked in crotchets) which permits a fusion of energy and expressive nuance: 'Tempo à la Brahms!'

The music of Mozart has all too frequently been sacrificed at the altar of what Casals termed 'systematic speed'. Casals' choice of tempi for the Symphony No. 29 provided an unforgettable music lesson. He took the first movement in accordance with the composer's Allegro moderato indication, his relaxed alla breve beat allowing ample time for the singing line to be set forth in all its warmth and grace.

Ex. 150

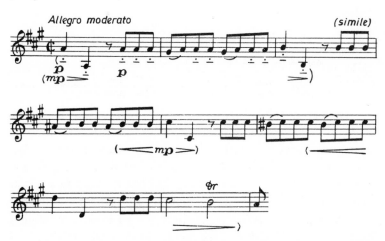

A vitally energized upbeat signalled the Finale and established at once the sturdy character of the 6/8 pulsation, reminding us that vigour is not synonymous with celerity:

Ex. 151

As Chaucer declares:

> Ther nis no werkman, whatsoevere he be,
> That may bothe werke wel and hastily.

One often hears the first movement of Mozart's 'Linz' Symphony (Allegro spiritoso, C) taken alla breve. Casals conducted it in four, giving time for the first theme to be phrased with incomparable loveliness (see Ex. 23).[1] However, when he took the last movement of Mozart's 'Prague' Symphony in two beats per bar rather than the customary one beat, I found his choice of tempo to be unduly slow. Casals explained that he felt that the triplet figure (Ex. 152) possesses a singing quality which precludes a faster tempo.

Ex. 152

Among the most stirring memories of Casals as conductor were his readings of Mozart's slow movements. No music is more expressive of fathomless sorrow than the C minor movements of the Piano Concertos in E♭, K. 271 and K. 482, and of the Sinfonia Concertante for Violin and Viola. Casals brought to these works the full depth of his humanity. Immersed in their mood of aching melancholy, he let them sing without hurry, sustained by the surety of his insight into the shaping of phrases.

---

[1] '*Spiritoso* is to say that one has to play with understanding and spirit ... the mean between quick and slow.' – LEOPOLD MOZART.

Expressive of an entirely different mood, the slow movement of the 'Haffner' Symphony flowed in a gracious *andante con moto*, while the second movement of Haydn's 'Surprise' Symphony was conceived in crotchet beats.

Whenever Casals performed the music of Haydn, one felt the existence of a special kinship between interpreter and composer. Both were of simple background; each had learned to express the fullness of his nature; neither had lost contact with the elemental vitality of the earth. One remembers Casals rehearsing such a dance as the Minuet from Haydn's Symphony No. 95:

Ex. 153

As he sat in his chair, his body would begin to sway from side to side, the alternating movement of his feet – as they came down on the first beat of every bar – communicating a primal rhythmic impulse, invincible and irresistible.

He played the Finale of Haydn's D major Cello Concerto with rustic lilt: 'not heavy – gay!' The tempo was not to be hurried: 'Six-eight – not two-four!'

Ex. 154

Nor was the robust, earthy side of Mozart to be neglected; it resounded in Casals' performances of the Minuets from the Symphonies Nos. 39 and 40, both of which (marked Allegretto) were taken, essentially, at one beat per bar. The former was resplendent with joy; 'Happy!' Casals shouted. The latter was intensely dramatic, with slashing accents upon the syncopations.

Ex. 155

The Minuet from the 'Haffner' Symphony was also played in a spirited 'one', the opening four bars brought together in a vivacious sweep.[1]

Ex. 156

Although Casals often expressed his concern over 'the modern tendency to play too fast', his performance of these minuets indicates that he did not hesitate to take comparatively fast tempi when they were appropriate to the musical context.[2] For example, he conceived the opening movement of Bach's Second Brandenburg Concerto as a jubilant celebration; this work, he felt, was meant to sound fast and he conducted it accordingly. By way of contrast, his performance of the Andante from Bach's Second Gamba Sonata (see Exs. 49a & b) had the quality of a pro-

---

[1] In a letter addressed to his sister, Mozart expressed surprise at the slow tempo in which minuets were performed in Italy.

[2] Reference has already been made to his spirited rendering of the first movement of Beethoven's Eighth Symphony.

found lamentation; there was no haste in the motion of quaver beats. So masterful was Casals' sense of the structure of the whole, so absorbing was his spiritual concentration, that the phrases unfolded in time units of enormous spaciousness, like the verses of a choral ode by Sophocles.

For Casals, the musical pulse was the organic heartbeat of a composition. He was able to integrate a manifold wealth of nuance into the framework of the main tempo. When he modified the fundamental speed, it was because of the intrinsic demand of the music.[1] Such a case is found in the Finale of Beethoven's A major Cello Sonata where Casals felt it necessary to give the second subject enough extra time so that it should not be robbed of tenderness. Each phrase played by the cello, he explained, must say 'I love you'. The piano, responding with increased motion, made bridges between these phrases. With the semiquaver figure the main tempo was fully re-established.

Ex. 157

[1] Wagner (*On Conducting*) makes a distinction between those allegros which should proceed in strict tempo and those innately subject to tempo modification.

The poetic content of the first movement of Beethoven's
Fourth Symphony was allowed to express itself in terms of slight
tempo fluctuations. Casals delicately restrained the tempo in the
transition to the second subject so as to arrive at a charming 'poco
meno mosso' without loss of continuity.

Ex. 158

In the midst of the development he again relaxed the pace. Each
chord entered like a sigh, the semiquavers trailing off unhurriedly.

Ex. 159

The passage took on a mood of sustained expectancy, as if an
ocean-going schooner were momentarily becalmed. The
vivacious *tempo primo* was gradually restored during the transition
to the recapitulation.

Certain compositions are, of inner necessity, subject to *tempo
rubato* not only within the phrase, but over extended sections
where the pulse-beat must yield with subtle flexibility to the

need of the phrases to move freely. Such elasticity of tempo is called for in the first movement of the Schumann Cello Concerto and Wagner's 'Siegfried Idyll', to give but two examples.[1] In Casals' performances these modifications of tempo were never arbitrary, never disturbing to the unity of the whole. They were carried out with consumate skill, ever in keeping with Bruno Walter's maxim: 'apparent continuity' of tempo. Casals would sometimes comment: 'There is an art to not playing in tempo – an art which one has to learn, which one has to *feel*.'

This art reached its summit in Casals' performance of the Trio from the second movement of Brahms' E minor Sonata:

Ex. 160

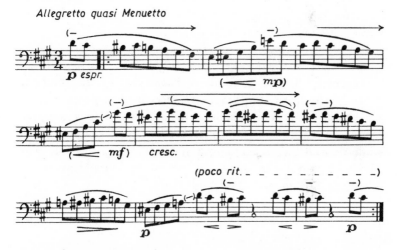

Any semblance of strict metronomic regularity was set aside, the rhythmic values responding instinctively to the expressive urge of the melody. The notes were free of constraint, yet inextricably related to one another by that sense of proportion which was a secret of Casals' artistry.

[1] In Bars 75–90 of the Wagner work Casals told the orchestra: 'I change constantly the tempo – follow me; follow me!' In the same passage Toscanini had said, 'Look me – watch stick – tempo always change.'

When teaching a large-scale work where numerous changes of tempo are required, Casals frequently reminded his students that they must take into account the relationship between one tempo and the next. Especially problematical in this regard is the Dvořák Cello Concerto. In the first movement Casals cautioned against taking the second subject too slowly (see Ex. 218). It should be only a little broader than the main tempo. Similarly, there is a tendency to transform the sustained A♭ minor passage into a lento (see Ex. 86). On such occasions Casals would remark: 'There is nothing worse than having to wait for the end!'

Throughout the second movement, a clear crotchet pulse was to be discernible. (Dvořák was careful to add to his Adagio: *ma non troppo*.) Reference has already been made to the need to maintain continuity in the transitional passages which occur within this movement.

The G major episode in the Finale (see Ex. 82) was not to be sentimentalized; Casals asked that the *Moderato* marking should be observed: 'It is a pastorale – classic and lovely.' Only in the coda was the rhythmic motion set free from any suggestion of pulse beat. The lyric statements of the cello were allowed to proceed in an improvisatory manner, the orchestra regaining tempo while the cello sustained its long notes. Thus was the solo cello allowed to express in all liberty the spiritual apotheosis of the concerto.

Casals would not wish us to forget that 'the silences are also music'. He advised the interpreter not to seek to minimize the effect of a rest; on the contrary, he should grant it its full due. If the line of feeling remains unbroken the silences will take on expressive intensity. This he called 'the art of the rest'. In Casals' hands such moments were spell-binding, a memorable instance occurring at the end of the introduction to the first movement of Beethoven's Fourth Symphony:

Ex. 161

Here, many conductors feel uncomfortable with the extent of silence which comprises nearly an entire bar in adagio; they tend to hurry it along. Casals made no apology for the length of this rest; he observed the full time indicated, letting the world stop to wait for the next crashing fortissimo.

There were quiet passages in Beethoven's cello sonatas during which the rests seemed absorbed with sustained tension, as in the Adagio from the Fifth Sonata, where the quaver rests led with halting steps from an already dark D minor into the impenetrable gloom of C♯ minor.

Ex. 162

In the concluding bars of the opening Adagio from his Symphony No. 39, Mozart introduces a mysterious passage built

from notes of long duration, in which time glides so slowly as
barely to move at all. Casals did not quicken the pulse beat here
as many conductors do. Each note, sustained to the full, trans-
ported us over a bridge of infinite poignancy, pointing the way
from darkness to light. The rests were expressions of eternal
longing; they traversed the space separating earthly sorrow from
heavenly consolation.

Ex. 163

I am reminded of the haunting moment during the first act of
Chekhov's play *The Seagull* when an unexpected quiet settles
over the stage. All is perfectly still until someone sighs, 'The
angel of silence has flown over us.' Casals was right to insist that
we accord 'the art of the rest' a meaningful place in our consideration of time relationships.

In the preceding chapters we have observed Casals' way of
granting to every note its inevitable role in a cogent design; his
insistence that each of these designs be articulated in such a way
as to imprint itself upon the ear unmistakably; his manner of re-
conciling the free and strict aspects of rhythm through 'fantasy
with order'. It is now time to look in greater depth at the
problems of string playing, giving our consideration to the means
– among them intonation, tone colour, vibrato – by which the
string instrumentalist can further communicate the life of music
in its 'endless beauty and diversity'.

CHAPTER V

INSIGHTS FOR STRING PLAYERS

Intonation is a question of conscience.

STEPPING into the Memling museum in Bruges was not like entering any other museum. I had spent the morning strolling along the rain-washed streets of that ancient and beautiful city, immersed in the spirit of a past age, lost to the distractions and pressures of the twentieth century. Thus it seemed a most natural thing to walk into the twelfth-century Hospital of St. John and find there, in the chapter-house, the Memlings, so rightfully belonging. No sooner had I begun to study these exquisite works of art, wrought with such infinite care, than the custodian asked if I wished to borrow a magnifying glass. What a splendid idea! Under the glass, a new world met the eye, a world in which every segment of canvas revealed unimagined refinement, in which human hand and paintbrush had achieved a delicacy of nuance at which one could only marvel. I set aside the glass and each painting – now seen as a whole – seemed richer than before, pervaded with internal life hitherto unsuspected.

I am reminded of Bruges and its Memlings when I recall Casals' teaching. Like that thoughtful custodian in St. John's Hospital, he would offer a magnifying glass to his student – a lens which enlarged not space but time – the better to examine a fragment of a Bach suite: a single bar, or half a movement, played in slow motion so as to place under close scrutiny the phrase structure, the why and wherefore of every dynamic inflection, the precise extent of articulation easily overlooked in a more rapid tempo. Students are often urged to 'practise slowly', mainly to analyse technical difficulties. Casals' purpose was infinitely broader; by bringing an aspect of a composition into larger view, not only did he ensure maximum awareness of every interpretative requirement but he uncovered the deep roots of expression from which all music is formulated. To hear him thus play the opening statement from Schumann's Cello Concerto, elucidating in an adagio tempo the meaningful connection of each note to the other, the heartrending quality of every appoggiatura and syncopation, was unforgettable. When reintegrated into the original tempo, these nuances, now proportionately faster, retained the precise character which the slow-motion process had enabled us to perceive. Our experience in music was enhanced by a further dimension of depth and of clarity.

When we examine different aspects of Casals' approach to string playing, it should be borne in mind that we are considering fragments which reveal their full meaning only when restored to the whole.

'Intonation,' Casals told a student, 'is a question of conscience. You hear when a note is false the same way you feel when you do something wrong in life. We must not continue to do the wrong thing.' His assertion that 'each note is like a link in a chain – important in itself and also as a connection between what has been and what will be', applied as equally to intonation as to other aspects of interpretation. The notes of a composition do not exist in isolation; the movement of harmonic progressions, melodic contours and expressive colorations provides each interval with a specific sense of *belonging* and/or *direction*. Consequently, Casals stressed that the equal-tempered scale with its fixed and equidistant semitones – as found on the piano – is a compromise with which string players need not comply.[1] Playing in tune is therefore not a matter of adherence to intervals

---

[1] These remarks are also applicable to wind players and, not least, to singers.

based upon a pre-ordained mathematical formula; it is a dynamic process, expressing the organic relationship between notes in a musical context, which Casals termed 'expressive intonation'. The final judgement lies in the ever-sensitive ear of the musician.

Because it is a natural and instinctive response to music, expressive intonation is to some extent practised spontaneously by many musicians. However, few apply it with the comprehensive awareness that characterized Casals' approach. New students coming to Casals – most of them advanced, some already professional – would often have comfortable illusions shattered when their habitual intonation was challenged by his uncompromising ear. It was rare enough when Casals, beaming with delight, could announce, 'You play in tune!' For this reason a more detailed explanation should prove useful.

The principal challenge confronting the string player whose sensibilities have been dulled by the mechanical pitch produced by the piano is to establish the proper placement of semitones. Here we must distinguish between diatonic and chromatic semitones, the former being invariably characterized by a sense of connectedness which Casals likened to 'gravitational attraction'.[1] Casals considered the tonic, subdominant and dominant of a given tonality (the first, fourth and fifth degrees of a scale) to be points of repose to which the other notes are drawn. Thus, the principle of gravitational attraction is at work within each of the two tetrachords of which a scale is composed. The diatonic semitone within each tetrachord has a natural tendency to be drawn upwards: the third degree towards the fourth and, most particularly, the seventh degree – the leading note – towards the octave. The pitch of the leading note needs to be raised high enough for us to feel the inevitability of its resolution to the tonic.

---

[1] I define these semitones as follows: when two notes forming a semitone are written on different degrees of the staff (i.e. C♯—D) the interval is diatonic. When they are written on the same staff degree (i.e. D♭—D♮) the interval is chromatic.

If the semitones are placed higher, the intermediate tones are affected; they must adjust accordingly. Consequently the second and sixth degrees are inclined slightly upwards. In the D major scale, for example, the E and F♯ are drawn towards the G, the B and C♯ towards the D.

Ex. 164

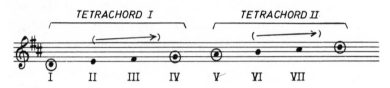

In minor scales the attractions are somewhat altered, yet always in accordance with the same principle of relating a note to its neighbours.

In performance these 'gravitational attractions' are anything but academic; they are a vital aspect of musical communication. Take, for instance, the opening melody of Mozart's Symphony No. 40.

Ex. 165

The first note (E♭), being the sixth degree of the G minor scale, has an innate tendency, in descent, to lean towards the D. To play this properly in tune the string player should – by design or intuition – slightly lower the pitch of the E♭, bringing it closer to the D. This can readily be tested by playing Ex. 165:

(i) on a stringed instrument with the E♭ slightly lowered, as described above;

(ii) on the piano;

(iii) again on a stringed instrument, matching exactly the intonation of the piano.

At this point it will be apparent that version (iii) is out of tune like a telescope not quite in focus; the E♭ has lost its expressive attraction towards the D and has become detached and impersonal.

Let us consider another passage, the second subject of the Finale of Beethoven's Third Cello Sonata:

Ex. 166

Here we are in E major. The D♯, as leading note, is drawn magnetically upwards towards the tonic E and must therefore be played slightly higher in pitch than the D♯ of the piano.

If we compare the E♭ in the Mozart symphony with the D♯ in the Beethoven sonata, we discover that these two notes are surprisingly different. Casals pointed out that under such conditions there may be as great a distance between E♭ and D♯ as there is within a semitone such as D♮—E♭.

The phrase which opens Mozart's String Quartet in E♭, K. 428, possesses five semitones: four diatonic and one chromatic.

Ex. 167

While the notes within each diatonic semitone are closely related to one another, the B♭—B♮, comprising a chromatic semitone, are not drawn together. The B♭, as fifth degree of the E♭ major tonality, is in a fixed position; the following B♮ is inclined away from the B♭ towards the C.

Similarly, in the opening theme of Schumann's 'Adagio and Allegro' Op. 70:

Ex. 168

the closer affinity exists not between the notes of the chromatic semitone E♭—E♮, but between the second and fourth notes which comprise the diatonic semitone E♮—F. (The intervening G is an appoggiatura which does not alter the fundamental attraction that draws the E♮ towards the F.)

These few examples, culled from endless possibilities, indicate the basis for the principle which Casals was to reiterate time and again: 'In general we are obliged to have the tendency to keep the half-tones close together.'

Occasional compromises will be inevitable owing to the exigencies of chordal fingering or in places where an open string has to function as the leading note. In the latter case, when possible, Casals stopped the string with the first finger, thereby improving both intonation and tone quality:[1]

Ex. 169   Schumann: *Cello Concerto,* 1st mvt.

The precise intonation of semitones will also be affected by the speed at which they are performed. Casals advised, 'In a relatively fast movement [i.e. when the specific semitone rela-

[1] See also Ex. 147.

tionships move quickly] we have to exaggerate still more the
closeness of the half-tones.' He demonstrated by playing the
following passage:

Ex. 170

(i) allegro, in which case the B♭ and G♯ are both drawn
    towards the A to the extent that the intervals approximate
    'an eighth of a tone'.
(ii) andante, requiring that the intervals – while narrower
    than those of the equal-tempered scale – should be a little
    less narrow than would be the case in the allegro.

When demonstrating a properly measured semitone, Casals
would sometimes exclaim, 'Isn't it beautiful!' And indeed it was.
The placement of intervals in meaningful relativity provides a
fundamental sense of well-being. The notes fall into place with
inevitability, thus gaining in vitality. Intellectual awareness, intuitive perception and critical listening all play a role in the
determination of the precise degree to which the instrumentalist
adjusts his pitch.

One does not have to look to Berg or Bartók to find challenges
to playing in tune. Although Bach's Sarabande from the C minor
Suite (see Ex. 171) is a work for solo cello without accompaniment, each note must be felt in accordance with the ever-present,
implied harmonic background. It falls all the more to the cellist's
responsibility to suggest these implications – by means of intonation – without supporting harmony. No placement of pitch can
be isolated from its brethren; no interval can be considered apart
from its gravitational tendency. Thus major and augmented
intervals will of necessity be widened, minor and diminished
intervals narrowed. Certain semitone relationships are intimated
even if not immediately resolved. For example, the A♭'s (sixth

degree of the tonality) in Bars 1–3 find their resolution in the G's which conclude the third bar. The B♮ (leading note) in Bar 2 looks towards the C in the fourth bar.[1] The depth of expression conveyed by this sorrowful piece in C minor is intrinsically related to the tension felt within the intervals. Expressive intonation, when observed continuously throughout a composition, becomes a foremost factor in the communication of emotional content.

Ex. 171

When teaching this piece – in slow motion – Casals commented, 'To play in tune is long, long work. You must never cease to observe, to educate and be severe with yourself.'

Casals considered it essential that expressive intonation be taught to string players from the beginning of their studies. He took endless trouble in retraining the aural sense and habitual finger placements of students who, since childhood, had unquestioningly applied piano intonation to their stringed instruments. 'The effects of any neglect of this kind at the beginning of studies . . . can affect a player through the whole of his career, however gifted he may be.' I once met the living proof of this statement in a cellist who was attending Casals' Berkeley classes – a performer not without talent but who had early on been brainwashed by equal temperament. Hearing Casals for the first time, she exclaimed, 'It is *soooooo* beautiful – but why does he play out of tune?'

---

[1] See also the relationship: D♮—E♭ in Bars 6–7; there are several such instances of delayed resolution in the second part of the movement.

Casals pointed out that when the cello is tuned in perfect fifths, the lower strings tend to sound too low in comparison with the upper strings. He advised tuning the C and G strings a bare fraction sharp, thus slightly narrowing the fifth between the G and D strings, achieving thereby an equilibrium between the extreme registers of the instrument. This tuning also has the benefit of drawing the lower notes of the cello into line with the equivalent notes on the piano which may otherwise, owing to equal-tempered tuning, be too sharp in comparison. He recommended that violinists follow the same procedure, i.e. tuning the two lower strings − G and D − imperceptibly higher.

Casals was of the opinion that, when a stringed and keyboard instrument play together, the discrepancy between expressive and equal-tempered intonation is easily tolerable. Except in unison passages, he believed it unnecessary and devitalizing for the string player to adjust to equal-tempered pitch.

The degree of bow pressure and the volume at which one plays are relevant to intonation. Where intensive bow pressure is indicated, the string will tend to sharpen and a necessary compensation must be made by the left hand.

Casals would tune his cello in mezzo forte so as to hear the natural sonority of the strings. But this was off-stage. Once on-stage he would, if necessary, brush the strings lightly with his fingers. 'Tuning with the bow disturbs the audience. They have nothing to do with the instrument.'

In previous chapters consideration has been given to the wealth of nuance which Casals believed to be inherent in all music. His bow communicated these inflections with the soaring power of song and the articulateness of speech. He brought to the art of cello playing a hitherto unimagined range of tone coloration. 'He was,' said Kreisler, 'the monarch of the bow.'

'To give variety with the bow!' Casals would exclaim, '− that is the natural thing.' He referred to the once-prevalent fashion of consistently using the full length of the bow as being 'against the requirements of the language of music' and 'contrary to the

economy of energy which a performance demands'. More
bluntly he said: 'It is a stupid idea.' Nor does music divide itself
systematically among a few basic categories of bow stroke:
spiccato, détaché, martelé, etc. The divisions are as subtle as
they are manifold and can intermingle within a single phrase. In
recording some instances of Casals' approach to bowing, I shall
not be providing a comprehensive list. My few examples should
be considered as illustrations of the cardinal principle: the bow
must always be responsive to the diversity of expression
demanded by the music.

In keeping with the special importance Casals accorded to the
articulation of the first note, he frequently utilized a technique
which young string players are often dutifully warned against:
the dropping of the bow upon the string. When announcing the
opening theme of the Dvořák Concerto:

Ex. 172

his bow would hover for a moment high in the air – like an eagle
watching its prey – before slashing upon the string with stunning impact. The arm movement, executed in one motion,
began with a vertical descent, suddenly curving to the side at the
moment of contact so that the string avoided hitting against the
fingerboard and could vibrate freely. The sound thus produced
was explosive without being harsh. So precisely did he judge the
natural weight of the falling bow that he obtained, as he occasionally put it, 'the greatest possible effect for the least possible
exertion.'

Casals showed a student how to express the dramatic opening
of Bach's Fifth Cello Suite:

Ex. 220

He gave great importance to the understanding of the harmonic context of each note. For instance, in Bars 5–6 of the above example, where a modulation leads from G major to E minor, he drew attention to the A at the beginning of Bar 5, this being 'the first note of the change of harmony; one imagines one hears the D♯ already sounding as the bass.' Here, he explained, as is generally the case where there is a modulation, the first note needs a little elongation: 'This gives the character of rubato – which is not a rubato – which is very agreeable. We must not hear one note after another like a machine.' When coming to the interval of the diminished seventh: he pointed to the expressive value of the C leading from the D♯ to the B; this was not to be considered as an inconsequential passing note. 'You see why it is necessary to make a profound study.'

Casals frequently drew attention to an extraordinary feature of this music: 'It is fantastic to think that with one note after the other there can be melody, the central voices and the bass all together. A wonderful polyphony – and this is an invention of

Bach. We have to give the proper expression to each voice.'
When teaching the Bourrée from the Third Suite, Casals would
first play the essential melodic line and then demonstrate how the
lower notes (indicated by the brackets below the staff) serve as
'complement and bass'; if they are given an importance equal to
that of the upper part, they become 'a repetition which harms the
melody'. He further differentiated these textures by playing the
lower quavers with spiccato bow strokes 'so as to have variety –
colour'.

Ex. 221

Similarly, in the Prelude to the Fifth Suite, he would elucidate
the polyphonic structure. 'All the entrances of this subject – in
piano, mezzo forte or forte – must retain this feeling' (of linear
polyphony).

Ex. 222

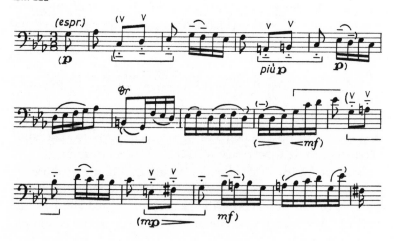

When performing the Courante from the Third Suite, Casals lightened the texture of the descending arpeggios by playing them 'off the string' in diminuendo. 'The purists are scandalized because I do that,' he said, adding sardonically: 'because it seems – it *seems* – that in Bach's time staccato didn't exist. But don't be afraid.'

Ex. 223

'That's beautiful, isn't it? Well, if it's beautiful, it's good.'[1]

'Bach was the greatest colourist!' Casals would exclaim. 'He loved colour. In the first prelude from the Well-Tempered Clavier he begins with only arpeggios – but what colour!'

Casals had often to remind his students that in each movement of these suites (excepting the preludes) Bach conveys this full range of expression through the medium of dance. Sturdy, robust, the natural rhythmic accents well marked, the dance character of these movements is not merely figurative but literal. In Casals' performance, most of these courantes, menuets, bourrées, gavottes and gigues could well have started feet tapping on any village green.[2] When teaching the Gigue from the Third Suite: 'This must give joy to everyone who hears it. No formality. *Rustic* – there is no place for niceness.'

[1] As was often the case, Casals, by trusting his intuition, came to conclusions which were later supported by musicological research. It is now known that staccato and spiccato bowings were employed by such eighteenth-century virtuosi as Tartini and Geminiani. As early as 1687 Jean Rousseau, in his *Traité de la Viole*, refers to the frequent use of 'rebounding bow strokes which are called "ricochets"'.

[2] Casals emphasized that within each suite there should be variety from one dance tempo to the next.

Ex. 224

Even the slowest and most meditative movement, the sarabande, was not to be entirely divorced from its rhythmic origin. 'A sarabande is not a romance or an adagio; it is a Spanish dance which used to be performed in the churches and is still danced in Sevilla.' Casals would indicate the steady, measured gait of the three crotchets in a bar, explaining, 'We must not be lost between one beat and another.'

Students often try to follow Casals in his variety of inflection without keeping in mind his insistence upon rhythmic continuity. Rubato, yes – but *within* the bar, without upsetting the dance character, and even then, a 'rubato which is not a rubato . . .'

The BBC once prepared a programme comparing the recordings of several cellists playing the Prelude to Bach's First Suite. Among these, Casals' reading was unique in its fullness of expression, its ability to let the phrases breathe. It was assumed that these attributes were a consequence of his having taken much more time than his colleagues. The stopwatch revealed otherwise; Casals' performance of this work proved to be nearly the fastest of all.

It is no easy task to bring to realization the manifold expressiveness of this music – its melodic, rhythmic and polyphonic properties, its strength of mood. The opening eight bars of the Courante from the First Suite provide a brief insight into the way in which Casals gave consideration to these various elements.

Ex. 225

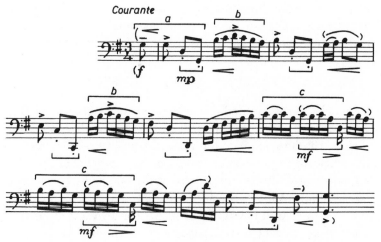

He began with a vigorous upbeat, absolutely in tempo. The downbeat was then marked with a decisive accent of the bow: 'Bite the string!' The dance was thus born to rhythmic life, the first beat of each bar receiving the primary accent; the third beat, a secondary stress. Casals asked that the upbeat be played 'on the string' with sustained tone. This for two reasons: 'It is the first note, which means the beginning of a melody'; and, when the upbeat is played tenuto, the staccato in the subsidiary voice (the quavers D–G) is heard as a contrast:

i.e. 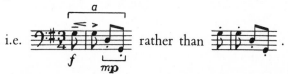 rather than

Casals went on to point out that, in figure (b), the third semiquaver requires a slight accent 'because it is the highest note and because it gives the third beat which is so necessary to mark the rhythm.' In figure (c) 'the same four notes, when played the second time, must be a little softer; in this way we avoid monotony and give value to the phrase that follows.' The upbeat to the final bar (the leading note F♯) was to be sustained as it leans towards the G at the bar line: 'We arrive at the confirmation of the tonality.' 'How beautiful is this music,' he exclaimed; 'how gay, how noble!'

Casals' performances and teaching of the cello suites over the course of nearly three-quarters of a century revealed their true greatness, gaining for them a permanent place in the repertoire and leading the way to a rediscovery of Bach by cellists in our time.

It must be borne in mind that in constructing a movement Bach depends not upon the juxtaposition of sharply contrasting themes, rhythms and moods that one frequently finds in music of the nineteenth and twentieth centuries, but upon the evolution of a fundamental thematic idea stated at the outset. As Furtwängler has written: 'With Bach, the entire potential development of a work is implicit in the subject as such.' The artistic realization of a complete movement is dependent in the highest degree upon the interpreter's ability to reveal the specific character of that subject.

We are here witness to a supreme creative power. These multitudinous themes of Bach — be they simple or complex in form, vivacious or serene in temperament — share a quality which we find also in Shakespeare: an uncanny sense of inevitability in the expression of something essential. (Indeed, Casals often drew an analogy between Bach and Shakespeare.) When interpreting these themes, we cannot separate their spirit from their form; we must experience them organically. When we re-encounter a work of Bach, as when we re-read *Hamlet* or *King Lear*, our perception of its meaning may be subject to change; we may render it differently, but never *less* meaningfully. When Casals interpreted Bach, there was no doubt about it: a concept was present. Every theme was marked with that distinctive commitment of insight and feeling, which the ancient Chinese called a 'heart-print'.

Take, for instance, the first movement of the Third Gamba Sonata, very often gone over briskly in a nondescript manner. Casals revealed the enormous power of expression in this work.

'This is not a gay thing – it is dramatic; we must feel the tragic character throughout.' He played in a moderate tempo that allowed one to sense the weight of the underlying quaver pulsation. The first two notes, he pointed out, are introductory; the semiquaver G is the real beginning of the theme. He brought to the motif ♫ ♪ a resolute strength.

Ex. 226a

The phrases which follow were played more lyrically; each up-beat was sustained in tone and intense in feeling.

Ex. 226b

In the concluding bars he gave dynamic inflection to the melodic rise and fall and underlined the agitated dialogue between the D's and E♭'s by means of a subtle rubato.

Ex. 226c

The Overture to the Second Orchestral Suite opens with an impassioned statement:

Ex. 227 .

Yet the following allegro section is usually played as a cheerful dance, quite detached from the mood of the preceding and following Lentement. Casals considered the fundamental character of the allegro subject to be determined more by the plaintive, melodic feeling inherent in the appoggiatura:

(reminiscent of Ex. 227) than by the rhythmic implication of the syncopation. He interpreted this as a tender melody, moderate in tempo, singing in texture. The second phrase was played a little softer than the first. Thus performed it was a song of sorrow, befitting its setting.

Ex. 228

How often have we heard the ritornello from the slow movement of the D minor Clavier (or Violin) Concerto rendered as a

series of unvaryingly uniform quavers! We will recall Casals'
having said: 'It is a general rule that repeated notes or a repeated
design must not be equal.' When interpreting this theme, he gave
expressive weight to the first note of each pair of quavers, the
second note subsiding as an expiration.[1]

Ex. 229a

Played in this way, the theme seemed transformed into a succession of sighs. 'Bach – the "cold Bach" – more than anyone, Bach
is human.'

Ex. 229b

That these notes held intense emotional significance for the composer is evidenced by the fact that Bach eventually incorporated
this movement into a cantata (No. 146), at which time he super-
imposed upon it a chorus set to the text 'Wir müssen durch viel

---

[1] Many present-day interpreters would think that they were 'romanticizing' Bach's
music by performing it in this manner. In fact, it was customary in the eighteenth century to play such groups of notes with expressive inequality.

Trübsal in das Reich Gottes eingehen' (We must pass through much tribulation to enter into the Kingdom of God).

When Casals conducted the St. Matthew Passion, he revealed how the ritornello to each aria conveys more than an indefinite impression of idealized emotion; it translates into a unique musical design the immediate intensity of feeling found in the text.[1] The aria 'Blute nur, du liebes Herz' (Only bleed, beloved heart) provides a characteristic example. Built as it is of syncopations, appoggiature and abrupt leaps, this theme communicates the presence of a grief so intense as to be experienced physically. Casals gave full expression to this daring musical language.

Ex. 230

The opening figure (*a*) was played as an imploring cry, falling off in diminuendo. The first appoggiatura within figure (*b*) began at a high point of expression, each descending sequence yielding in intensity; the phrasing was always:

[1] It was in his eighty-sixth year that he fulfilled his life-long wish to direct this masterpiece. While preparing the score he wrote to me: 'The more I work on it, the greater it becomes, and the more problems I find to render an honest and meaningful performance. I am so much in it that I cannot sleep at night with this wonderful music going through my head.'

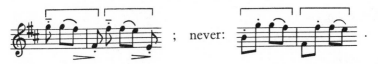

; never:

In figure (c) he gave dynamic contrast to the rise and fall in the chain of syncopations. Figure (d) ended in a diminuendo, bringing into bold relief the urgent forte of the final phrase (e), the expressive culmination of the theme. This music gave such a spontaneous feeling of sorrow as to seem woven from tears. 'Bach must be free,' Casals would say. 'When the purists hear me say you must play Bach like you play Chopin they are horrified. But I laugh at them. Nobody has arrived to the expression of Bach.'

Casals often spoke of the 'universality of Bach's art'. He would point out that Bach had not only assimilated the French and Italian styles. We find in his music other influences as well – the Hebraic:

Ex. 231 *Violin and Clavier Sonata No. 3*, 3rd mvt.

Ex. 232 *Solo Cello Suite No. 4*, Prelude

the Hungarian:

Ex. 233   *Solo Violin Sonata No. 1, 1st mvt.*

'Let us not forget that the greatest composers were the greatest thieves. They took from everyone and from everywhere.'

The worldly charm of dance rhythms, so often springing from foreign soil, is felt time and again in Bach's music, even when, as is often the case, the dance is not designated by name. The gigue-like allegro theme from the Overture to the Fourth Orchestral Suite falls into this category. 'With joy!' Casals exclaimed when rehearsing this work. He then proceeded to translate this word into an irresistible rhythmic lilt by means of relevant fluctuations in dynamic intensity (*a*). (An unusual feature of this theme is the displacement of the principal point of rhythmic stress from the first to the second beat.) The repeated D's (figure *b*) moved buoyantly towards the second beat in Bar 4.[1]

Ex. 234

Here, as so often, Casals drew attention to the enunciation of the first note. The Marlboro Festival Orchestra had begun the theme with enough élan to please any other conductor, but for Casals the upbeat sounded ever so slightly lazy. Although in piano, it

---

[1] Bach used this movement as the basis for the opening chorus of the Cantata No. 110: 'Unser Mund sei voll Lachens' (May our mouths be full of laughter).

was to have immediate, springing vitality. 'The first note is not
happy enough,' he remonstrated. After pausing momentarily for
dramatic effect, he continued: 'And also the second note sounds a
little sad.'

When rehearsing another gigue-like movement, the Finale of
the Third Brandenburg Concerto, Casals asked the instrumentalists who play the accompanying figure to give natural accents
to the main beats, while lightening the weight of the intermediate quavers:

Against this background, the semiquavers were to be played
melodically, with graduations of dynamic intensity corresponding to the curve of the phrase; the crescendo was not to be exaggerated: 'Without forcing – natural – lovely.' The result was an
entrancing fusion of dancing and singing.

Ex. 235

Bach often incorporates these two elements in a single theme.
When teaching the second movement of the First Gamba Sonata,
Casals showed how the first two phrases dance 'delicately, joyfully'. In keeping with the vivacious mood, Casals played the
rhythmic figure ♪♪♩ with a certain concision: 'It must not be

s.t

---

heavy – grazioso!' The concluding phrase, beginning with the upbeat, was to be sung upon expressively. 'The whole melody has an expansion of an octave and four notes,' he explained. 'You have to do something with that; otherwise it could be monotonous. When the phrase goes up, go up with your sound; then it becomes something complete.'

Ex. 236

Where there is a contrapuntal texture which contains both a subject of signal personality and distinctive countersubjects, Casals would carefully explain the specific characterization required for each component part. For example, he described, as follows, the four elements which comprise the fugal passage from the Third Orchestral Suite.

The Subject was to be played with singing bow strokes, 'sounding nearly legato'. This theme, Casals pointed out, is formed of three phrase segments, each consisting of six notes; each of these segments has an upbeat character. He sang the essential melodic notes – in quavers – indicating the increase of tension within each ascending interval of a third.

Ex. 237a

The highest note of each segment was to come as an expressive climax, but without accent; within that note itself there was to be a diminuendo, thereby giving the next phrase segment a softer point of departure: 'that is the economy'. Each crescendo came with increased intensity, so that all three segments combined into one melodic curve.

Ex. 237b

Countersubject I was to establish an immediate contrast in texture. These quavers — 'meno forte' — were executed with short bow strokes; each syncopation received a pointed accent followed by a rapid diminuendo.

Ex. 237c

Countersubject II was again melodic, played 'on the string', the dynamics following the melodic contour.

Ex. 237d

Countersubject III was not to be a monotonous repetition of quavers in a single sonority. Each phrase, always beginning with the second quaver, was to be felt as a series of upbeats and played with expressive 'portato' bow strokes:

Ex. 237e

Every motif thus contributed its individual vitality to the whole. The result was a wonderful polyphony, informed with organic life.

Ex. 237f

A word should be added about the interpretation of dotted
rhythms in Bach's music. Casals avoided making a blanket
application of any theoretical formula. Where the melodic line
requires breadth and nobility (as in the slow sections of the over-
tures to the orchestral suites) he did not alter the printed note-
values; where the rhythmic feeling demands a certain vivacity (as
in the Polonaise from the Second Orchestral Suite) he extended
the length of the dot in order to vitalize the relationship between
the short and long notes (see Chapter IV). The precise extent to
which the dot was elongated was variable, dependent upon his
instinctive response to the phrase in question. For this reason he
did not refer to 'double-dotting'; a more appropriate term would
be 'over-dotting'.[1]

When performing dotted rhythms in a movement in which
triplets are a prominent feature, Casals applied the principle of
over-dotting, preferring it to the more customary solution of
compressing ♩. ♪ into the triplet figuration: ♩ ^{3} ♪. Thus, in the
last movement of the Fifth Brandenburg Concerto, Casals
quickened the semiquavers, providing a lively contrast to the ensuing triplets.[2]

Ex. 238

As each musical conception of Casals was deeply experienced, he
generally remained within its framework whenever returning to
a given work. Yet the journey of interpretation, so well charted,
traversed a thousand times over, never ceased to yield fresh in-

---

[1] This term is used by Robert Donington in his book *The Interpretation of Early Music*.

[2] Opinions differed even in the eighteenth century in regard to this matter. C. P. E.
Bach favoured the assimilation of the dotted note-values into the predominant triplet
rhythm, whereas Quantz expressed the view which Casals was subsequently to adopt:
'. . . when one of the parts has triplets against which the other part opposes dotted
notes, it is necessary to sound the little note which follows the dot, only after the third
note of the triplet, and not at the same time with it.'

sights; a detail or a larger aspect would reveal itself in a new light. For this reason he could not be coaxed into editing Bach's cello works for publication. He advised his students to consult the source closest to the original (the copy made by Anna Magdalena Bach) where, unencumbered by intervening editorship, the master's notes perpetually invite interpretative rediscovery. He himself resisted, and would have his pupils resist, the tendency to be inextricably bound to preconceptions, however well founded.

Casals' way of varying his approach to the last movement of the Fourth Brandenburg Concerto is illustrative of this flexibility. The principal subject of this movement is usually played in a straightforward, rather angular manner. Thus it came as a revelation to me, when Casals conducted this work in Prades (in 1953), to hear the violas announce this theme in an unhurried tempo, with tender expression.

Ex. 239

Each subsequent voice entered with singing quality (the overall sonority gradually increasing in intensity). If this subject fell graciously upon the ear, it was due to more than beauty of tone production. The first figure (a) was played with smoothly connected strokes of the bow, figure (b) in a contrasting dance-like quasi staccato. Moreover, within figure (a), in keeping with the resolution of the suspension, the G–F♯ came in a natural diminuendo; this left room for an increase in sonority to the A which stands at the high point of the melodic curve. So interpreted, the theme was divested of inelasticity and became eloquently expressive.

It was a sultry morning in Puerto Rico, eight years later, when I next heard Casals conduct the Fourth Brandenburg Concerto.

As he slowly made his way towards the podium, he seemed a very tired old man. Yet at the moment when he gave the upbeat for the first movement (Ex. 240) he was utterly transfigured. It was Moses smiting the rock. 'Life, life, life!' he cried, as the joyous notes sprang forth. 'Always try to find variety – it is the secret of music.' His exuberance of temperament had an electrifying effect upon the musicians.

'All three notes are different,' he explained to the violins who were to affirm the jubilation of their ascending line (*x*) with a crescendo. When playing figure (*y*), the flutes were to sustain the quaver which comes at the top of the phrase (just before the bar line); the element of song was not to be excluded from this predominantly dance-like passage.

Ex. 240

'Do not keep the same sonority in forte,' he demanded. 'Every part must be interesting. We must play the music with *character*.'

Ex. 241

A passage which can easily sound stilted was greeted radiantly: 'Like a lovely dance – with fantasy; Bach – charm, charm!'

Ex. 242

All of these diverse inner phrasings were encompassed within the vivacious but unvarying lilt of the unifying (one beat per bar) rhythmic pulsation.

The second movement ('andante – not adagio') became under his direction a lament – 'always singing and molto espressivo', the first of each group of two slurred quavers slightly emphasized but 'without exaggeration'. 'Doloroso, doloroso,' Casals implored. 'There is no passion in what you do. Give more and more every time.' His voice rose in a fierce crescendo: 'I hate monotony; I HATE IT!'

Ex. 243

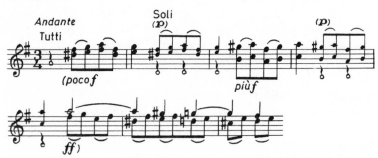

When Casals turned the page of his score to the last movement, I awaited the entrance of the violas, recalling the wonderful way in which he had interpreted this theme in Prades. But then, to my surprise, he brought his baton down upon the first note with incisive force. Rather than conceiving a lyrical line, he

* In Ex. 242 we observe another case of a dual impulse occurring during the course of a suspension (see Ex. 36). Casals asked for this note to begin with a diminuendo; at the last moment a crescendo was to lead over to the following bar.

demanded vigour and strength. Each of the two minims was
rendered forte, the first being given a diminuendo so as to
bring the articulation into bold relief. (The subsequent phrasing
remained as before.) The tempo was vivacious, the mood
irresistibly jubilant.

Ex. 244

Of these two ways of interpreting the theme of the last movement it is impossible to assert that only one is correct. The essential point is that in each case the theme possessed *character*. But, of
the two, I must confess my preference for the former, which
remains in my mind as one of the loveliest things I have ever
heard played.[1]

Casals would be the last to want us to regard his insights into
Bach as being rigid formulae. They were the expression of his
questing spirit; the revelation of a voyage of discovery which he
began alone at the age of thirteen; the ecstatic consequence of his
having dared to trust to his feelings.

Once, when teaching the Bach suites in a master class, Casals
played two different movements for his students. The first was
the Sarabande from the Fifth Suite in C minor. 'You see,' he said,
'this is such a profound expression of pain, like the music from
the Passions.' He then played the Gigue from the Third Suite in
C major. 'Nothing is more gay,' he exclaimed, 'nothing is more
healthy, more wonderful! In the same way that we give that profound feeling of pain, let us also give that profound feeling of
joy. You mustn't remain in the middle. Play frankly! Don't be
afraid. Give what is due to the music and to Bach.'

[1] The reader may compare both versions, as recorded by Casals in Prades (1950) and
in Marlboro (1964).

CHAPTER VII

A CASALS REHEARSAL: THE PASTORAL
SYMPHONY

Molto espressivo! How beautiful it is – the illumination of nature...

THIS book has concerned itself with the principles of interpretation fundamental to Casals' music-making. I should
now like to provide a sustained glimpse into the workings of
Casals' musical mind as it applied itself to the re-creation of a
familiar masterpiece. For this purpose I invite the reader to attend
a Casals rehearsal of Beethoven's Pastoral Symphony. My notes,
taken during several rehearsals at the Casals and Marlboro
Festivals, have been brought together into one continuous commentary.

Casals shared with Beethoven a profound love of nature. One
day, when I was speaking with Casals on the terrace of his home
in San Juan, our conversation was interrupted by the raucous
squawk of a seagull. He pointed to the bird enthusiastically and,
after observing it for some moments, commented, 'You never
lose time when contemplating nature.' He went on to speak of
his daily walks on the beach, of the dogs who befriended him on
these excursions, of the ever-changing beauty of ocean and sky.
He was at one with Beethoven in believing that nature is the best
'school for the heart' and, like the composer, to whom every tree
seemed to say 'Holy! Holy!', the manifestations of nature were,
for Casals, reflections of the divinity.

His performance of the Pastoral Symphony – infused with joy
and reverence – was one of the most exquisite treasures he gave
to us. It was never recorded. Although this loss is irreparable, in
noting here Casals' interpretative indications, something of the

letter and, perhaps, spirit of his conception may be preserved. The limitations of this book preclude a complete description; I have omitted, for instance, Casals' numerous references to orchestral balance, confining my commentary to matter of enduring validity. For the benefit of those readers who do not have access to a score, I have provided musical quotations to illustrate each point.

Whether shaping a phrase with his bow or with his conductor's baton, Casals was always conveying his essential ideas about music. 'Making music is what interests me,' he said, 'and what better instrument is there than an orchestra. . . . It is the supreme medium for anyone who feels music deeply and wants to translate the form and shape of his most intimate thoughts.' He brought to a Beethoven symphony the same degree of care and devotion which he accorded to a solo cello suite by Bach, rehearsing in minute detail until every note was imbued with internal life and had taken its place in the overall design. We find in Casals' performance of the Pastoral Symphony a summary of his principles of interpretation.

FIRST MOVEMENT

Awakening of Cheerful Feelings upon Arrival in the Country

Allegro ma non troppo
Casals' tempo: ♩ = c. 108–112
Bars

1–4   'We must play the beginning simply,' Casals explained; 'it is only an indication of what is to come.' Time and again he went over these opening bars, pruning away excess – redundant vibrato, undue bow pressure, exaggeration of accent.

1   The cheerful mood was to be established with the *very first note*: 'It must not sound sad!' He cautioned the

violins to avoid an inadvertent crescendo from the A to

the B♭, i.e.  ; 'Do not force the tone.'

'The second note,' he pointed out, 'is not short; it has
no dot over it' (a fact to be kept in mind throughout
the movement). The bass was to diminish right away:

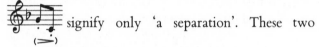

2   Casals explained that dots, in Beethoven's time, did not
necessarily imply staccato; those under the G and C

 signify only 'a separation'. These two

quavers are innately 'poco diminuendo'.

3   Bar 3 was played without crescendo, the semiquavers
coming without heaviness 'in a natural rhythm', a bit
late and quickened.

4   The fermata [pause] took on its inherent grace through
a diminuendo 'at once', going to the infinite. Casals
conceived the opening four bars as divided naturally
into two segments of two bars each, a nuance more to
be felt than emphasized. Patiently and surely, he
worked until the melodic contour revealed itself –
pristine and radiant – in all simplicity.

5   The new phrase was invested with immediate singing
quality, each note well articulated by the fingers.

6   Throughout the movement the figure of two semiquavers was to retain its lively rhythmic character.

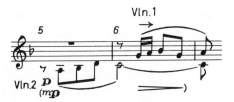

11, 13   Beethoven has written forte in Bar 11 and, again, in
          Bar 13. In order to avoid repetition of the same
          sonority and to enhance the sense of expansiveness,
          Casals differentiated these dynamics as follows:

9–11   The crescendo attained to poco forte.

12   This bar, yet light in texture, was set apart as a separate
          segment.

13   The reoccurrence of the forte was now stronger and
          'più espressivo'.

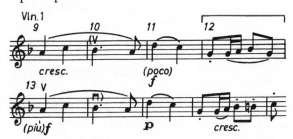

28–30   The oboist, as solo player, can lend further expressive-
          ness to the theme; Casals asked that the second quaver
          in Bar 29 be clearly enunciated to render the beginning
          of the melody distinct; the notes at the top of the
          phrase were to be delicately elongated.

37–53   Here, as so often, Casals freed the melodic design from
          the tyranny of the bar line. In those cases where the
          natural stress should fall upon the second crotchet beat,

he cautioned, 'Avoid accenting the first note of the bar.' The accents which he requested within the bow-

ing slurs, e.g.  , are

of a compensatory nature; they serve to clarify the first note of the semiquaver figures which, otherwise, are all but lost to the ear of the listener. In this case Casals counselled, 'Force the bow!' (i.e. exaggerate the accent to ensure intelligibility). 'Variety in forte,' he demanded. 'Not just *one* forte!'

53–57 *et seq.*   In contrast to the preceding tutti, the texture was now more fluid and relaxed: the woodwind, non staccato, came like lovely murmurings with a diminuendo extending not only up to but *through* the seventh quaver; the violins – 'simple, natural, unforced'.

64–66   The repeated figure in the violins was not to remain on
one dynamic level, but to be played 'with less and less
sonority'. The violins then made the slightest break
before Bar 67, as if to catch their breath in happy an-
ticipation of the phrase to come.

67–74   The principal theme, Casals indicated, is that which
begins in the bass; it rises and falls in waves, seeking
completion in its higher notes. The quaver figure
(violins), although also expressive, is by comparison
'ornamental'. Lighter in weight, it falls in a
diminuendo from its highest note.

75–82   The parts are now reversed, each wave retaining its
et seq. characteristic ebb and flow as indicated above. The
diminuendo within each phrase imposes a natural
gradation upon the growth of dynamic intensity. In

this way 'the phrasing brings economy to the crescendo'.

93-96   Maximum articulation is required! Note, in Bar 93,
the decrescendo on the dotted crotchet, the better to
clarify the notes which follow. The violins and violas
were urged to play the semiquavers incisively 'with
strong, clear fingers'.

97–100   The melody here is usually performed in one line. Casals, however, felt it in three waves. He gave expressive emphasis to the first note of each bar, letting the other notes subside in diminuendo. 'When we break the phrase in this way, we must do it tenderly, tenderly . . .'

107–115   The woodwind and strings, in turn, gave contour to the variations of the above theme.

The violins were asked to play 'on the string', in the upper centre of the bow, 'big – but not jagged', the melodic notes brought into relief.

115–119   Every part had independent life.
et seq.

123–125
et seq.
The melodic pattern, consisting of whole-bar rather than half-bar units, retained its form throughout the diminuendo.

147–150
The reappearance of a theme is not to be treated as a mere repetition of what has been heard before. Casals addressed the clarinettist: 'There is more beauty to be found here. The F is more important; this brings the natural loveliness. But play without forcing at all – dolce, dolce ...'

151–152
et seq.
No passage is more susceptible to routine performance than these long stanzas woven from strands of motivic repetition. Casals brought to bear his insight into the character of each figure; the music suddenly became startlingly fresh and alive. The new version of the motif taken from Bar 2 was given natural shape by means of a tiny pointed accent and diminuendo. The violas and cellos were not to be neglected: 'Even here, there is room for ups and downs.'

155–162   Sustained notes, taken in turn by the first and second
et seq.   violins, now add their voices to this woodland
            counterpoint. 'When there is a long note, it must be
            heard from the beginning.' Each was to commence
            with a quick, vibrant accent (followed by a rapid
            diminuendo) and then gradually increase in intensity.

175–178   'Give form to the tutti!' Casals demanded. He pointed
out to the woodwind that if the quaver at the end of
each bar is played in diminuendo, the succeeding
dotted crotchet 'comes as a novelty'. The violins were
to sing their semiquavers 'like a sustained note, avoiding stringent force'. Now, in fortissimo, 'every note in
the bass must be marked'. There was to be an overall
crescendo. 'Monotony is no music!'

193–196   This figure, taken in turn by the second violins and
cellos, was espressivo, attention being given to the first
of the little notes (F♯) that is should 'not be swallowed'.
The reiterated quavers were played with rhythmic lilt.

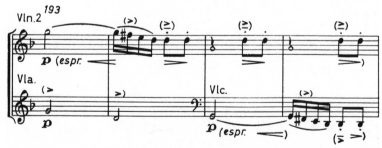

241–246   Casals heightened the effect of the *dolce* (marked by
Beethoven in Bar 243) by indicating that the flutes

should play *giocoso* in the two previous bars, with a diminuendo at the end of Bar 242, then suddenly with warmth of tone in Bar 243. The *dolce* catches us by surprise – a typical Casals characteristic.

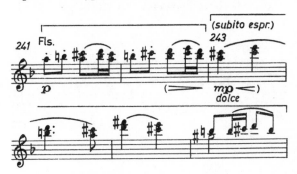

255–258
et seq.
The mood of a passage determines the expressive character of a sforzando. Here the *sfp*'s throb quickly, with sensitivity.

263–266   Casals indicated the points of tension and relaxation which give this theme its inner structure. Note the crescendo within the quaver E (last note, Bar 264) as it leans into the sforzando, and the subsequent decrescendo to the first quaver of Bar 266, at which point Casals insisted: 'No accent here; it is ugly!'

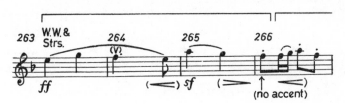

267–275   Each successive sforzando came with increased intensity, the last (Bar 275) being the strongest of all:
'*Arrive!*' Casals called out.

275–278   The first note of each triplet was to be clearly articulated, the decrescendo carefully gradated.

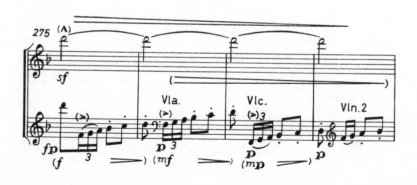

279–282   We have now come to the recapitulation. Upon
return, the first subject is richer in associations; it
evokes a deeper response within us than it did upon
first encounter. Thus Casals urged the second violins
and violas to play 'with more expression' and allowed
the adorning high C of the first violins a poco crescendo.

282–288   The beginning of the trill was to receive an accent: 'It
gives character to the long note.' The little notes

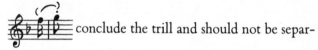 conclude the trill and should not be separ-

ated from it. (The separation comes after the first
quaver in Bar 285.) The violins were to play 'with the
sound of a flute – not hard – pianissimo, dolce'.

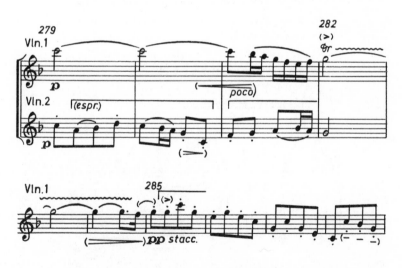

293–300   In the first four bars Casals asked the woodwind to sing
out nobly. In the variation of the phrase (Bars
297–300) the strings were to respond with a heartfelt
'echo'.

As the remainder of the recapitulation concerns itself with material already commented upon, I shall now pass to the coda.

422–425   These four bars – 'rustic and strictly in tempo' – resounded in a robust forte (Beethoven has not marked fortissimo).

426–427   'Contrast – *molto più dolce.*'

428–432   Owing to its long slurs and symmetrical rhythm, this
et seq.   passage (a variant of Bars 115–119) can easily sound
monotonous. By giving subtle dynamic emphasis to
certain notes (marked by brackets) Casals brought
contour to the lyrical line.

448–451   'Don't play notes – play a melody,' Casals beseeched.
'On the string – cantando, cantando!'

456–467   Now, at the climax of the movement, Casals opened
his arms in that wonderful gesture of his which seemed
to embrace the spirit of every man and woman in the
orchestra. 'Molto espressivo!' he exclaimed. 'How
beautiful it is – how beautiful – the illumination of
nature . . .'

476–486 The clarinet gaily and lovingly shaped the design:
et seq.

492–498 The violin figure (and that of the flute in the subsequent bars) was to be very delicately phrased in the following pattern:

The two final chords, coming in diminuendo, communicated a deep composure.

SECOND MOVEMENT

Scene at the Brook

Andante molto moto
Casals' tempo: ♪· = c. 44
Bars

1 *et seq.* It would be hard to forget that old man, indicating to his string players the unceasing movement of the flow-

ing stream, swaying gently as if he were rocking a
cradle with all the tenderness and serenity of a mother's
love; such was the repose he evoked, so tranquilly did
the bow strokes flow together. 'Use much bow,' he
counselled, 'but very little pressure. We must avoid
accents. When changing the bow, eliminate the stop
and the crescendo.'

1–4   The opening crotchet (played by the first violins) was
not to be taken for granted. Casals sang it roundly and
nobly. 'It announces "Beethoven".' As Casals uttered
the composer's name, it communicated a tangible
quality of feeling, an entity in itself, needing no further
elaboration, recalling to mind Schumann's comment:
'BEETHOVEN – what a word – the deep sound of the
mere syllables has the ring of eternity.'

Against the unchanging background of quavers, the
melody was given time to express its full lyricism. The
first note of the second bar was played – 'not as
written' – but more spaciously than notation can indicate. The turn, in Bar 3, was not hurried.

5–6   The first note of the ornament in Bar 5 was articulated
with greatest care. Beethoven has indicated crescendi in
both Bars 5 and 6. In Bar 5 the crescendo extends to
forte. In order to give variety and to render the end of
the phrase more exquisite, Casals requested 'only poco
crescendo' in Bar 6.

7 *et seq.*   Each accompaniment figure was instilled with a life
of its own. Casals asked the first violins to articulate
clearly the beginning of every trill. The other string
players were to give expressive emphasis to the notes
of melodic significance within the semiquaver
figuration.

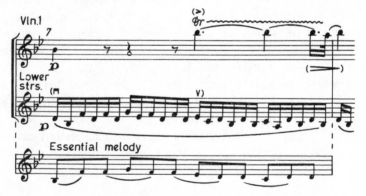

11   Even in the general crescendo, each trill was characterized by a diminuendo.

13–14   The first B♭ is the beginning of a melody. The violins were to commence with warm tone, make a diminuendo, then a crescendo on the second note. The reiteration of the B♭'s gained in meaning through the release and renewal of intensity.

17–18   Repetitions in the same sonority were anathema to Casals. Each accent had to come with less tone, the final crotchets with individual diminuendi.

19   This passage was rehearsed at least a dozen times. The violins were to linger ever so slightly upon their initial quaver. The first note of the turn was to be well pronounced, the subsequent quaver F again espressivo. 'It is cold!' Casals entreated. 'Don't be afraid to take time. It must sing so tenderly!' The semiquavers – 'not too short' – were gently pulsating, the crotchets always tapering off in diminuendo.

23–28   The first violins were phrased as follows, with consummate grace:

29   Casals always stressed that, within the arc of an overall crescendo or diminuendo, the inner phrasings must retain their shape. Here he emphasized the high note of each group of descending semiquavers, giving importance to the underlying 6/4 pulsation. The intermediate notes, coming in diminuendo, were not to be lost to the ear.

30, 33   The solo flute and bassoon, respectively, were to give expressive inflection to the melodic rise and fall.

39   The groups of quavers followed one another like rap-
turous sighs: 'Each time as though a new breath is
taken! But don't forget that the second note [i.e. the
second quaver within each slur] must also be heard and
must not be short.' Diminuendo poco a poco.

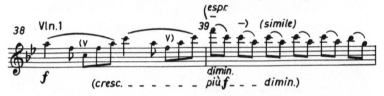

47–50   Casals imparted to the orchestra the spontaneity of
feeling characteristic of his own cello playing; each
successive upbeat was instantly vibrant and singing.

50–51   He urgently addressed the first violins: 'Give time for
et seq.   the first note!'

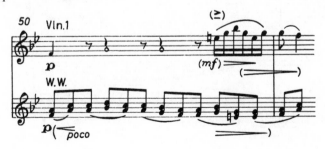

58–60   The principal theme, taken here by the oboe – subsequently by the clarinet (Bar 69) and flute (Bar 91) – is normally performed in strict time. For Casals there was 'more to be expressed'. He urged these solo woodwind to 'play freely'. 'We will keep time; you do as you wish.' He counselled these players to anticipate their entrances, coming in a little sooner than written so that the semiquavers would have more time in which to sing. The appoggiatura at the bar line was to be delicately lingered upon. Such rubato eludes precise notation. It could be approximately expressed as follows:

To hear this melody, liberated from constraint, soaring freely over the regular movement of semiquavers,
was indescribably moving.

62–63   Casals pointed out that the dotted crotchets in the first
violins, although an accompaniment, should none the
less be played with melodic insinuation.

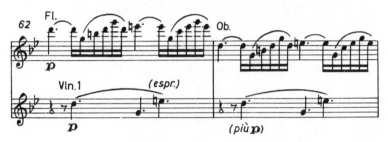

65–66   The flute and oboe were to trace the melodic curve
with dynamic inflection.

79–80   The violins were asked to begin in mezzo forte so as to
give increased dimension to the subsequent decrescendo.

81–82   Here the orchestra attained the most intimate pianissimo. The notes seemed divested of material weight;
they were transparent, floating.

125–127   In order to enhance the soaring quality of their long
et seq.   B♭, the violins were requested to play on the E string
(the sonority being brighter than on the A string) with
a great increase of vibrato. The turn was given time to
sing. The concluding semiquavers, although in
diminuendo, were not to be too soft too soon.

129–131   The rarest of qualities is the ability to be simple.
Flautists, like string players, tend to protect their right
to use vibrato. How enchanting it was, therefore, to
hear the solo flute, in response to Casals' request, begin
'without vibrato, simply, like a bird'.

131   Casals considered the printed notes here to be no more
et seq.   than approximations of natural rhythms. The solo oboe

and clarinet were urged to play slightly quicker than written: 'Like bird calls.'

In contrast to some great German conductors' rendering of this bird dialogue, in Casals' performance one had the impression of a cuckoo saying 'cuckoo' – not of Goethe saying 'cuckoo'.

132–133   In giving the birds back their voices, human feeling responds all the more deeply. Casals spoke in a hushed voice: '*Extase . . . extase . . .* how wonderful is the nature . . .' The orchestra played with reverence.

136–139   Beethoven has now marked a *pp* which Casals observed with care. Beginning with the utmost intimacy, the phrase was passed from instrument to instrument in one unbroken line of expression, each upbeat warmer than the last, the clarinet being allowed a crescendo a half bar prior to the place indicated in the score, the better to bind together the whole.

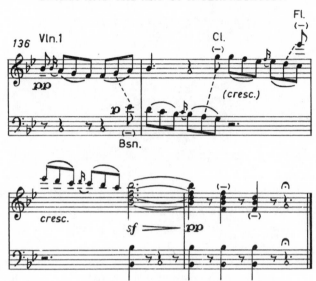

A movement of unsurpassed loveliness was thus crowned with what Shelley has called the halo of beauty.

THIRD MOVEMENT

Happy Gathering of the Country Folk

Allegro
Casals' Tempo: ♩. = c. 88
Bars

1–8   Casals conveyed at once his inimitable feeling for the character of a dance. His tempo – a moderate allegro – established a balance between the motion of whole-bar beats and the vitality inherent in each individual crotchet. While unhurried, the dance was yet light and gay: '*Tempo giusto* – but not heavy'. The delicately accented grace notes enhanced the vivacious lilt.

9–16   Casals drew attention to the lyric contrast provided by
        the answering theme; Beethoven has indicated dolce
        and 'it should sound dolce'. The quavers were to be
        played 'a little faster than is the custom'. The phrase
        was to end in diminuendo; none the less, the con-
        cluding quavers (Bar 15) 'must be heard'.

63–66   A diminuendo on every dotted minim (without stop-
        ping the bow between the strokes) 'gives more
        strength to each sforzando'.

91–98   It is a rustic dance; even so, the quavers (Bar 93) were
et seq.   to 'sing melodically'.

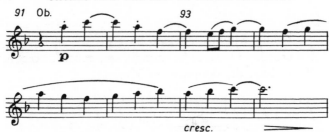

165–168   Casals marked the accents of the 2/4 dance with that
et seq.   primal energy which sprang from the peasant earth.
            He conceived the pulse in whole-bar units ($\downarrow$ = c. 68).
            His baton slashed – uncompromisingly, violently –
            upon each sforzando. ('Diminuendo each time in the
            bass!')

            One felt the feet of the country folk stamping upon the
            ground. Brueghel the Elder has depicted such a scene
            in his 'Wedding Dance in the Open Air'.

203–206   After the second fermata [pause] Casals allowed a
            caesura, thereby increasing the sense of expectancy
            before the return to Tempo I.

213–221   The quavers were to be drawn into relief – articulated boldly within the legato bow strokes. In Bar 218 the crotchet C was to be strongly emphasized, asserting, as it does, the dominant of F major.

FOURTH MOVEMENT

Thunderstorm

Allegro
Casals' tempo: ♩ = c. 156
Bars

1   There was no break between movements. The rumble of distant thunder came upon us unexpectedly.

Rather than conducting in the alla breve to which we have grown accustomed, Casals felt the pulse of this movement in crotchet beats. If he resisted making an effect through sheer speed, he conceded nothing in the way of vitality. His four beats per bar were so strict and exacting as to transmit an unrelenting impulse to the motion of the storm. The pianissimo was taut and

agitated; the fortissimo, fierce and concise. Every small
rhythmic unit became intensely alive.

3–6   Casals immediately addressed the second violins: 'Play
et seq.   with great excitement . . . as if the peasants were saying
to one another, "we must go home – something is
going to happen".'

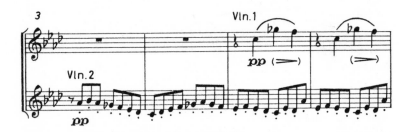

Every quaver conveyed a sense of presentiment. The
mood of nervous haste thus generated gave a greater
impression of hurry than simply playing the notes at a
faster speed.

19–20   The lower strings and woodwind have only two bars
in which to build up to the sudden outbreak of the
storm. 'As much crescendo as possible!' Casals shouted.

21–28   The storm was unleashed in full fury. It raged in a for-
et seq.   tissimo that was massive – but not formless. By means
of incisive accents and dynamic inflections (as in-

dicated below) its contour became apparent, standing
out in all clarity.

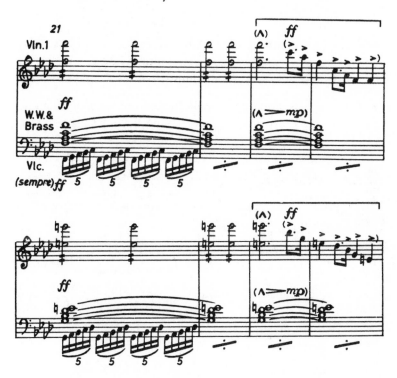

41–42   In Casals' tempo, the agitated semiquaver figures
et seq.   gained in intensity through increase in intelligibility.

43–44   Even in the impassioned sweep of the storm, every
et seq.   chord was to be balanced. 'We must hear all the notes
clearly; otherwise the harmony is not complete.'

56–61   Casals' phrasing brought increased interest to the violin
          line by delineating its motivic structure.

95–99   The syncopation was accented with the force of a
et seq. whiplash. The quavers which immediately follow
          were given clear articulation. The crescendo rose im-
          petuously.

119   The storm begins to subside; sempre diminuendo is
et seq. marked in the score. As it is eleven bars before piano is
          indicated, Casals asked that the decrescendo be gradu-

ated so as not to arrive at this piano too soon. The strings were to begin in the full intensity of their fortissimo, the violins accenting each upbeat, the bass line expressively declaimed.

130–136 The cellos and basses brought clarity to the groupings of semiquavers by distinctly enunciating the first note of each crotchet beat.

146–150 Casals now conducted in minims, the oboe and second
et seq.   violins singing serenely.

154–155 The solo flute was allowed a poco ritardando.

FIFTH MOVEMENT

Shepherd's Song: Happy and Thankful Feelings after the Storm

Allegretto
Casals' tempo: $\downarrow$. = c. 60
Bars

1–4   With the dissolution of the storm, the clarinet entered – 'dolce, as if from far away' – giving at once the flowing tempo for the last movement. Casals asked that each of the first two bars recede in diminuendo. Bars 3 and 4 were gone over lightly in one unit.

9–16   The first violins now commenced their melody of thanksgiving. 'Molto legato,' Casals entreated, directing that the quaver which concludes Bars 9, 11 and 13 be sustained in tone and connected with as smooth a bow change as possible to the note that follows. String players are inclined to take for granted their ability to play legato, but it was only after careful rehearsal, producing sensitive listening on the part of the violin section, that Casals could announce: 'That is beautiful; that is a *song*.'

Casals' performance of this movement conveyed not only its glory of melody, but also its vitality of rhythm. 'Six-eight – not two-four!' was his insistent demand. Where the sixth and third quavers possess an upbeat quality (e.g. ♪♩ ♪♩) they were always to be energetic, lively and strictly in time – whether played in forte or piano. Elsewhere, when appropriate, Casals gave lilting emphasis to the two main beats within the bar: ♫♩ ♫♩ . One experienced here, as in Casals' performances of Bach, an interaction of expressive song and vivacious dance. The vein of deep sentiment that runs through the movement was not allowed to subjugate the rhythmic pulse, thus becoming sentimental; it was embraced within the dance and thereby raised to the ecstatic.

17 *et seq.* The reiterated semiquaver pattern was to be given
25 *et seq.* rhythmic definition. Casals asked the violins to accent the first and fourth quaver beats.

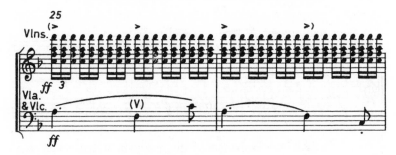

32–33   'Do not come late with the second note,' Casals warned. 'It must not sound heavy!' Quaver and crotchet were decisively accented. Each of the first two crotchets had a diminuendo to enhance the articulation; the third, a crescendo so as to bridge over to the C which crowns the phrase.

34   The violins proclaimed their upbeat with the most vital of accents.

42–45   The semiquavers were to be full of energy, but absolutely without rallentando. The *mf/cresc.* gave to the violin line a renewal of impetus, at the same time allowing the bass to come through more clearly. The long notes in the bass were to be played in diminuendo – the better to hear the beginning of the next phrase.

46   Here an even higher point of intensity was reached, the
      semiquaver A accented and tenuto.

50–53 The notes marked piano begin new melodic waves;
       they were to be immediately vibrant.

54–56 'Not lazy! – one, two, three, four, five, six! We must
       not lose time between the beats.'

64–71 For Casals, a repetition in music signalled a new experi-
       ence of feeling; he embraced the reappearance of the

principal theme with heightened emotion. The dynamics were shaped in response to the rise and fall of the melodic line. The violins were not to be shy of their upper notes (the C's in Bars 64, 66, 68); they were to bring soaring completion to the crest of each phrase. Using his baton as he would his bow, Casals ardently caressed the shape of the melody. 'Don't be afraid to express what you feel. *Every phrase is a rainbow.*'

78–80   'Six-eight': the quavers were to be equal to the crotchets in vigour and decisiveness.

80–82
et seq.   In accordance with the lyrical mood of the woodwind subject, the *sfz* was 'warm', not harsh, the upbeats sustained – but in tempo.

95–98   Even in this intimate and delicate pianissimo, the
tempo was to be maintained; the bass marked each
pizzicato, emphasizing the pulsation with rhythmic
exactitude.

99–100   The dance lilt was irresistible – the violins lightly
et seq.   stressing the first and fourth quaver beats, the bass
vitalizing the upbeats.

117–118   The violins were to play their exquisite variation of the
et seq.   principal theme with as much singing quality as possible – but 'lightly', without forcing the bow.

125–129 Casals asked the violins not to remain at one dynamic
et seq.   level; they were to follow the design.

148–151 In the mounting crescendo, Casals indicated that the
         second quaver of each group be played tenuto, with
         ever-increasing emphasis.

190   The impassioned line of the violins retained rhythmic
et seq.   shape.

219–222 The bass marked a titanic world dance: the notes were
et seq.   forged of iron, the line rising in a crescendo in a
         mighty upward swing, the staccato upbeats coming
         like hammer blows. The woodwind, brass and upper
         strings sustained their sonority, incomparably majestic,
         with the grandeur of an organ.

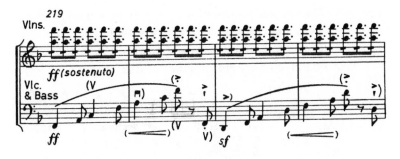

237–244   The strings now sang quietly, their sonority taking on
an inward tenderness akin to the voice of Casals' cello.
The tempo was delicately restrained (not the drastic
slowing-down one often hears). Casals gave individual
contour to the two-bar phrases, letting each one fall
away in diminuendo. Bars 241–244 were then bound
together in a single span. The concluding semiquavers
were allowed to sing without hurry. The beauty of
such music-making cannot be conveyed in words, nor
the beauty of feeling; this was a moment of benedic-
tion.

245–246 The orchestra again took up the dance – fully '*a tempo*'
– the quavers accented with rustic vigour.

247–248 The woodwind now played with gentle rubato in
contemplative remembrance of Bars 243–244.

249–252 The string and woodwind choirs, in turn, sighed farewell, the long notes decreasing in intensity.

260–263 Casals reminded the string players who accompany the
gently receding horn call, 'Even though you play
pianissimo, it is still a melody.'

263–264 The *ff* quaver was to be short, the crotchet long –
'with a natural diminuendo'.

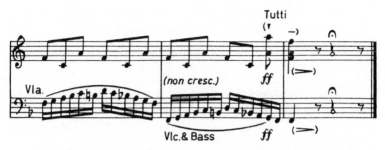

The last rehearsal had come to an end; yet for a moment no one moved. The reverberations of the music's spirit lingered on like ripples which persist long after a stone has been cast into deep water. Casals sat in meditation, his eyes closed. Deeply moved, he gave voice to his emotion: 'What a wonderful gift Beethoven has given to us!' He rose from his chair – again an old man – and wearily, but resolutely, strode off the stage.

EPILOGUE

In music, in the sea, in a flower, in a leaf, in an act of kindness . . . . I see what people call God in all these things.

CASALS held the fragile piece of paper in a hand that trembled not with age but with emotion. 'It is a wonderful thing to realize,' he said. 'Here Beethoven has written the first sketch for the Ninth Symphony. Before this, there was nothing; then, from the silence, came these notes — no more than a hint, a mysterious beginning. And from this smallest particle of thought that great work came to life. That is truly a miracle. This document is my most precious possession.'

I did not know then that this would be my last visit to Casals. My wife, daughter and I had arrived at his home late one afternoon and were greeted at the door with characteristic graciousness by his wife, Martita. There, at the far end of the room, we saw Casals at the piano. A door near him opened out towards the ocean. Only two sounds were heard: the music of Bach and the ceaseless rhythm of the waves.

Casals rose at once upon seeing us. The warmth of his greeting made me feel that our visit was not an unwarranted intrusion. Meeting our ten-year-old daughter for the first time, he expressed delight upon hearing that, in keeping with her name Pamina, she was studying the flute. 'The flute!' he exclaimed joyfully; 'I too once played that instrument and, as a child, I was particularly enraptured by the piccolo.' He spoke of his early years spent in the Catalan village of Vendrell and showed us, from among his mementoes, a large photograph of men and boys standing on each other's shoulders in a 'human pyramid', reaching the height of seven men. 'See what we do in my village!' Casals said, beaming with pleasure. 'Not even the circus people are as skilful as the peasants.'

We spoke of Spain – of the Feria of Seville in which the whole population, including tiny children, joins in spontaneous dance; of Cordoba, with its maze of quiet streets and shaded patios. Casals leaned back in his armchair; 'Cordoba is beautiful, beautiful,' he sighed. But his mood changed when he spoke of the Spanish civil war. Deeply affected by these reminiscences, he closed his eyes in meditation and said in a trembling voice: 'Thank heaven for music – and for nature.'

He told us of his playing two preludes and fugues from the Well-Tempered Clavier 'every day of my life; I love all the music, but I could not begin the day with another composer. Bach showed us what music *is*. First comes Bach – then all the others.'

Casals then brought out his treasures – a page upon which Mozart had written the conclusion of the third act of *The Marriage of Figaro*, the manuscript of Brahms' String Quartet in B♭ major, the sketch for the Ninth Symphony . . .

When we touched upon a problem faced by many musicians, namely stage-fright, he shook his head resignedly. 'For eighty, for eighty-five years – ever since I began to perform – I have lived with this. Many children are not nervous when they play in public, but I suffered when I was a child and I suffer even today when I must give a concert.'

I asked him whether he thought it advisable to give children simple pieces by Bach and other masters to play as soon as they are ready for them, rather than having them wade through a morass of inferior music. Casals wholeheartedly supported this idea and pointed out that Bach wrote such fine pieces for his own children. He embraced our daughter and told her of the wealth of beauty there is in music and how much she had to look forward to.

'I have had an idea,' he said to us, 'a plan for the education of children. I have spoken of it to important people and they say: "It is so simple, yet we have never thought of it." It is this: as soon as the child can understand the meaning of a word, he should be told that this word represents a miracle. When we speak of the eye, we should explain what a miracle it is to be able to see. We should explain what a miracle it is to be able to speak. What a marvel are our hands! When the wonder of each word has been made clear, then every child should be taught to realize: "*I* am a miracle – and *he* is also a miracle. I am a unique being; there never has been a person like me since the beginning of the world – nor will there be until our world comes to an end. And he, too, is unique and will be so until our world will end. Therefore, *I cannot kill him* – and *he cannot kill me.*" Only in this way can we do away with the impulse for wars. At school they teach that two plus two equals four. That is not what life is all about.'

As Casals uttered the words 'I am a miracle – and he is also a miracle,' he struck his hands to his chest. His blue eyes shone with indescribable radiance. He experienced fully the marvel of which he spoke. Looking into those eyes, I thought not of the frail body which contained them but of the transcendent spirit which resided there.

He continued: 'Real understanding does not come from what we learn in books; it comes from what we learn from love – love of nature, of music, of man. For only what is learned in that way is truly understood.'

'I cannot believe that these marvels which surround us – the miracle which is life – can come from nothingness. How can something come from nothingness? The miracle must come from somewhere. It comes from God.'

Later, when we were about to depart, Casals gave a final embrace to each of us. 'When you reach my age,' he said, 'anything can happen any time; I am prepared for it. So I love all the more every beautiful thing. How moved I am to be among my friends.' We protested that we were the grateful ones, but in vain; he would have none of it. As we left, he stood in the doorway waving farewell, perhaps sensing that we would not meet again.

The next day, as I looked out at the ocean, the waves seemed to melt into the eyes of Casals, and the eyes back into the waves. I felt that the expanse of sea, the arc of sky, the world of nature and humanity surrounding me had become a vast concert hall in which sounded the resonance of his soul.

PRINCIPAL REFERENCES

Bach, Carl Philipp Emanuel, *Versuch über die wahre Art das Clavier zu spielen.* Berlin 1753, Part II Berlin 1762. English version: *Essay on the True Art of Playing Keyboard Instruments.* Trans. and ed. W. J. Mitchell, Norton, New York 1949.

Barbirolli, Sir John, quoted from *Casals* by D. Wheeler, prod. C. Venning. BBC broadcast, London, September 1975.

Boult, Sir Adrian, 'Casals as Conductor', *Music and Letters*, vol. IV, April 1923.

Casals, Pablo, *Conversations with Casals* [recorded by] José Maria Corredor. Trans. André Mangeot, Dutton, New York 1956; Hutchinson, London 1956.

'Las Memorias de Pablo Casals' as told to Thomas Dozier, *Life en Español*, 4 May, 18 May, 1 June 1959.

Cardus, Sir Neville, *The Delights of Music.* Gollancz, London 1966.

Cherniavsky, David, 'Casals's Teaching of the Cello', *The Musical Times*, vol. 93, September 1952.

Couperin, François, *L'art de toucher le clavecin.* Paris 1716, 1717.

Cramer, Carl Friedrich, *Magazin der Musik.* Hamburg 1783.

Czerny, Carl, *Über den richtigen Vortrag der sämtlichen Beethoven'schen Klavierwerke.* Vienna 1842. Ed. K. H. Füssl and H. C. Robbins Landon, Universal, Vienna 1963.

Deutsch, Otto Erich, *Franz Schubert: Die Dokumente seines Lebens.* Munich, 1914. English version: *Schubert, A Documentary Biography.* Trans. E. Blom, Dent, London 1946. American edition: *The Schubert Reader.* Norton, New York 1947.

Donington, Robert, *The Interpretation of Early Music,* Faber, London 1963.

Eisenberg, Maurice, in collaboration with M. B. Stanfield, *Cello Playing of Today.* Lavender, London 1957.

Flesch, Carl, *The Art of Violin Playing* (2 vols). Trans. F. H. Martens, Carl Fischer, New York 1924–1930.

Furtwängler, Wilhelm, *Gespräche über Musik.* Atlantis, Zurich 1948. English version: *Concerning Music.* Trans. L. J. Lawrence, Boosey & Hawkes, London 1953.

Geminiani, Francesco, *The Art of Playing on the Violin.* London 1751. Facs. ed. D. Boyden, Oxford University Press, London 1952.

Grove's Dictionary of Music and Musicians. Macmillan, London 1878–89, 1904–10, 1927–8, 1940, 1954. American edition: St Martin's, New York.

Hind, Pamela, 'Casals as Teacher', *The R.C.M. Magazine*, vol. 46, 1950.

Jeans, Sir James, *Science and Music.* Cambridge University Press, London 1937.

Kirk, H. L., *Pablo Casals.* Holt, Rinehart and Winston, New York 1974; Hutchinson, London 1974.

Lehmann, Lotte, *More than Singing.* Trans. F. Holden, Boosey & Hawkes, London 1945.

Liszt, Franz, *Gesammelte Schriften.* Leipzig 1880.

Mozart, Leopold, *Versuch einer gründlichen Violinschule.* Augsburg 1756. In translating excerpts the author has consulted: *A Treatise on the Fundamental Principles of Violin Playing.* Trans. E. Knocker, Oxford University Press, London 1948.

Mozart, Wolfgang Amadeus, *Letter to his sister,* 24 March 1770; *Letter to his father,* 26 September 1781. *Mozart: Briefe und Aufzeichnungen Gesamtausgabe,* vols 1 and 3. Ed. W. A. Bauer and O. E. Deutsch, Bärenreiter, Kassel 1963.

Nettl, Paul, *Beethoven Encyclopedia.* Philosophical Library, New York 1956.

Quantz, Johann Joachim, *Versuch einer Anweisung die Flöte traversiere zu spielen.* Berlin 1752. Translations to which the author has referred: *On Playing the*

Flute. Trans. and ed. E. R. Reilly, Faber, London 1966. Excerpts trans. R. Donington, *The Interpretation of Early Music. ed. cit.*

Rousseau, Jean, *Traité de la viole.* Paris 1687.

Schumann, Clara, *Tagebuch.* February 1854.

Schumann, Robert, *Neue Zeitschrift für Musik.* Leipzig, October 1835, February 1841.

Schweitzer, Albert, *J. S. Bach* (2 vols). Paris, 1905. Trans. E. Newman, Breitkopf & Härtel, London 1911.

Shakespeare, William, *Hamlet.* Ed. J. Dover Wilson, Cambridge University Press, London 1934.

Shaw, George Bernard, article appearing in *The World,* 24 December 1890. Included in *Music in London 1890–94 by Bernard Shaw,* vol. 1. Constable, London 1932.

'Shakespear: A Standard Text', letter to *The Times Literary Supplement,* 17 March 1921. Included in *Shaw on Shakespeare.* Ed. E. Wilson, Dutton, New York 1961.

Stanfield, Milly B., *The Intermediate Cellist.* Oxford University Press, London 1973.

Stravinsky, Igor, and Craft, Robert, *Themes and Episodes.* Knopf, New York 1966.

Suggia, Guilhermina, 'Violoncello Playing', *Music and Letters,* vol. II, April 1921.

'A Violoncello Lesson: Casals's Obiter Dicta', *Music and Letters,* vol. II, October 1921.

Thayer, Alexander Wheelock, *The Life of Ludwig van Beethoven* (3 vols). Ed. H. E. Krehbiel, The Beethoven Association, New York 1921.

Tosi, Pier Francesco, *Opinioni de' cantori antichi, e moderni.* Bologna 1723. English version: *Observations on the Florid Song.* Trans. J. E. Galliard, London 1743.

Vaughan Williams, Ralph, *The Making of Music.* Oxford University Press, London 1955. Included in *National Music and other essays.* Oxford University Press, London 1963.

von Tobel, Rudolph, *Pablo Casals.* Rotapfel, Zurich 1941.

Wagner, Richard, *Bericht an Seine Majestät den König Ludwig II., von Bayern über eine in München zu errichtende deutsche Musikschule.* 1865. English version: 'Report concerning a German music school to be established at Munich'. Trans. E. Dannreuther, included in *On Conducting,* Reeves, London 1940.

Letzte Bitte an meine lieben Genossen. Bayreuth, 13 August 1876. Reproduced in *Wagner* by Hans Mayer, Rowohlt, Hamburg 1959.

Über das Dirigiren. 1869. English version: *On Conducting. ed. cit.*

Walter, Bruno, *Von der Musik und vom Musizieren.* Fischer, Frankfurt 1957. English version: *Of Music and Music-Making.* Trans. P. Hamburger, Faber, London 1961.

INDEX TO MUSICAL WORKS

Page numbers in italic indicate musical quotations.

GENERAL INDEX

Agogic accents, 81
  examples in various contexts, 16, 24–
    25, 35–36, 81–83, 181, 183, 185
Appogiature
  articulation of, 114–115
  dual impulse, examples of, 29
  expressive significance of, 39, 83, 102,
    150, 152–153
  phrase continuity, 29, 42–43
Articulation
  of accents, 50–55, 63, 163, 174, 191,
    192, 200–201
  analogy to speech, 50–52, 55, 63
  of appoggiature, 114–115
  bringing melodic notes into relief, 171,
    179, 182
  of repeated notes, 56–58, 117, 183, 197
  of short notes/ornaments, following
    long notes, within legato slur, 56,
    58–61, 63, 75, 168, 170, 174, 182,
    183, 190–191, 193, 196
  of trills, 123–124, 177, 182
  see also Bowing: attack; Finger per-
    cussion; First note; Left-hand piz-
    zicato

Bach, Anna Magdalena, 160
Bach, Carl Philipp Emanuel, xi
  on dotted rhythms in triplet passages,
    159n.
  dynamic nuances in his performance,
    18n.
  on expression, 18
  on rubato, 80n., 85n.
Bach, Johann Sebastian, 3, 208, 209

his art
  analogy to Shakespeare, 148
  dancing and singing elements, 154–
    156, 160, 161, 162, 199
  distinctive character of themes, 148–
    158, 160–163
  of contrapuntal voices, 155, 156–
    158, 161
  expression related to text, 152–153
  transformation of instrumental
    works into cantatas, 151–152,
    154n.
  its expressive range, 140–141, 163
  national styles, 153–154
  variety of colour, 145
interpretation of his works
  Casals' conceptions vs. prevalent at-
    titudes, 141, 145, 151, 153
  Casals' flexibility, 159–160, 162–163
  comparison with interpretation of
    Chopin's music, 153
  dotted rhythms, 159
  historical misunderstandings sur-
    rounding Bach interpretation,
    138–141
  see also Index to Musical Works: Bach,
    Suites, Violoncello Solo
Barbirolli, Sir John, 129
Bartók, Béla, 107
Beethoven, Ludwig van, xii
  love of nature, 164
  Schumann on, 181
Berg, Alban, 107
Bergonzi-Gofriller cello, 133
Boccherini, Luigi, 6

Boult, Sir Adrian, xii
Bowing
attack, 51, 78, 110–113, 147
bow as servant of music, 110, 121
change of bow stroke
on long notes, 114
while preserving legato, 42–43, 114,
181, 198–199
relatedness to vibrato, 134–137
repeated notes, variety in, 115–117
tone colour, its relation to speed, pressure, placement of bow, 120–121,
136–137, 181, 203
variety in textures, 109–110, 113, 144–
145, 147, 155, 156–158, 160
see also Articulation
Brahms, Johannes
tempo related to unit of musical pulse,
89–91
on Bach Gesellschaft, 139
British Broadcasting Corporation, 146
Brueghel, Pieter, the Elder, 192

Cardus, Sir Neville, 12–13
Chartres Cathedral, 88–89
Chaucer, Geoffrey, 92
Chekhov, Anton, 100
Chiaroscuro, 60
Ch'i-yün, 1–2, 14
Chopin, Frédéric, xii, 153
rubato of, 85
Chords
building of, 122–123
variety in interpreting, 123
Couperin, François
on rhythmic flexibility, 80n.
on notation, 70
Cramer, Carl Friedrich, 18n.
Czerny, Carl, xii
on Beethoven's playing, 72–73

Diminuendo
as bringing clarity to:
accents, 50–55, 63, 163, 174, 191, 192,
200–201
repeated notes, 56–57, 183

short   notes/ornaments,   56, 58–60,
75, 170
syncopations, 62–63, 157–158
bringing economy to a subsequent
crescendo, 23, 31, 63, 157–158,
160, 169–170
going to the infinite, 117–120, 166
lightening long accompaniment notes,
61–62
note endings, 117–120, 166, 168, 183,
206–207
gradation of phrase endings, 64–66,
184, 185, 188, 191
gradation of long diminuendi, 176,
185, 196–197
Donington, Robert, 159n.
Dynamic nuances, their relevance in
various contexts
general guiding principles, 20–21
long notes, 20, 26–29, 41, 46–47, 173,
177, 206
melodic curve, some typical examples,
15–16, 20–26, 33–37, 39–41, 46–49,
142–143, 149–153, 154–158, 167–168,
169–170, 175–176, 179–180, 184–185,
202
range of forte/piano, 20, 21, 28, 55
relativity of dynamics, 65–67, 187
repetitions in music, 20, 21, 151
analogy to speech, 29, 49
note repetitions, 20, 21, 30–31, 41,
151, 154, 157–158, 168, 183
phrase repetitions/sequences, some
typical examples, 20–22, 32–37,
39, 45–46, 147, 150–153, 157–158,
162, 183, 184
see also Phrase spans
see also Diminuendo

Eighteenth-century performing practice
bowing, 145
lack of expressive markings in scores, 7,
15–18, 49, 142
dotted rhythms, 71, 159n.
dynamic nuances, 17–18
expressivity, 7, 17–18, 151n.